THE LIBRARY OF
THE FUTURE

THE LIBRARY OF THE FUTURE

Alternative Scenarios for the Information Profession

BRUCE A. SHUMAN
Wayne State University
Detroit, Michigan

1989
LIBRARIES UNLIMITED, INC.
Englewood, Colorado

LIBRARIES UNLIMITED, INC.
P.O. Box 3988
Englewood, Colorado 80155-3988

Library of Congress Cataloging-in-Publication Data

Shuman, Bruce A.
    The library of the future : alternative scenarios
for the information profession.

    Bibliography: p. 127.
    Includes index.
    1. Library science--Forecasting. 2. Information
science--Forecasting. I. Title.
Z665.S485   1989   027.4   89-2466
ISBN 0-87287-656-X

Cover: Illustration by Frank R. Paul, "City of the Future," *Amazing Stories*,
August 1939. Photograph reproduced courtesy of Smithsonian Institution
Traveling Exhibition Service.

TO

Bek, Ben, Josh, Mom ...
and
Pammus Alabamus

Table of Contents

Preface

My interest is in the future, because I am going to spend
the rest of my life there.

— Charles F. Kettering

Originally, this was going to be a book about the future of libraries, any
kind of library, all kinds of libraries. It wasn't until the author was well along
in his research and first-draft writing of the book that he realized that the task
he had set for himself was not only gargantuan, it was virtually impossible. It
is the author's conclusion that it would take several thousand pages, or
perhaps a multivolume work, to do justice to the twofold task of providing an
adequate discussion of futuring methodology and a discussion of the future of
the library in all of its aspects.

Consequently, the author decided that rather than attempting to deal with
the future of all kinds of libraries in some superficial (and occasionally
unknowledgeable) manner, he has elected to deal in depth with the one type of
library he knows best from personal experience, the public library. This should
serve the dual purpose of providing a book which is both relatively concise and
informative, while insuring that the author knows what he's writing about.

The problem is that nobody really knows what he or she is writing about
when writing about the future. All we can do is follow accepted practices, spin
our fantasies, and then sit back and see if future developments bear us out or
make our predictions and projections into applesauce.

Therefore, the scope of this work will be the future of the public library,
the time frame will be the next twenty-five or so years, and the principal
technique will be the scenario. The reader is invited to ponder the scenarios in
this book, view them as possible alternative futures for the public library,
consider their implications, and notice carefully decision points at which other
directions might have been chosen. Remember that at any point along the way,
scenarios of the future can be changed and none of these has to happen. It's
only the past we can't do anything about. If you don't like these scenarios,
write your own, better, scenarios, and work hard to make them come true.

In doing some rather extensive reading for this exercise in speculation, the author ran across the following passage in the introduction to a book on business forecasting. In it, M. D. Kirby offered the following disclaimer:

> In Dante's *Inferno*, soothsayers and other futurologists are consigned to Malebolge, the eighth of nine circles of the Inferno. They are lumped together with pimps, flatterers, hypocrites, those who cause divisions, and liars. Their punishment is to have their heads reversed. Being deprived of the power to see before them, they are constrained to walk backwards for eternity. Fearful, lest the spirit of Dante inflict such a dread punishment on me, I propose to avoid speculation about the future.[1]

While Kirby is prudent and cautious in feeling that speculation concerning the future is rash, even dangerous, the present author, whether through folly or boldness, intends to do a lot of speculation about the future of libraries in this volume. Those fearful of Dante's shade coming to them in the night and readjusting their heads are advised to stop reading now and turn their attention to other matters. As Dante tells us, this warning is inscribed in the great gateway over the concentric rings of hell, "Lasciate ogni speranza, voi ch'entrate!" (Abandon all hope, ye who enter here). For the intrepid, take a deep breath and proceed at your own risk.

NOTES

1. M. D. Kirby, "The Morning Star of Informatics Law and the Need for a Greater Sense of Urgency," *Government Publications Review* 12 (May/June 1985): 203-14.

Acknowledgments

The author gratefully acknowledges the contributions of the following, who granted, or gave information leading to the granting of, rights and permissions for the use of the illustrations that appear in this work:

- The Bettman Archive, New York, New York.

- Daniel Fields, World Future Society, Bethesda, Maryland.

- R. Craig Gauld, Cableshare, Inc., London, Ontario, Canada.

- Willis W. Harman, Institute of Noetic Sciences, Sausalito, California.

- Lane Jennings, World Future Society, Bethesda, Maryland.

- Steve Justice, Creative Art Service, Dynamic Graphics, Inc., Peoria, Illinois.

- William L. Renfro, The Policy Analysis Co., Inc., Washington, D.C.

- Jeffrey Smith, CBS, Inc., New York, New York.

- Vicky Smith, *The Bulletin of the Atomic Scientists*, Chicago, Illinois.

- Hilary B. Thomas, Videodial, Inc., New York, New York.

- Melanie J. Wolfe, The National Museum of American History, Washington, D.C.

Illustration courtesy Clipper Creative Art Service,® copyright Dynamic Graphics, Inc., Peoria, Illinois.

1
Everybody's a Futurist

The past is gone, the present is full of confusion, and the future scares hell out of me.

—David Lewis Stein

HOW THIS BOOK CAME
TO BE WRITTEN

When J. C. R. Licklider, who was not a librarian but a psychologist, published *Libraries of the Future* in 1965, it received a generally favorable critical reception and very limited sales figures. For years, the author has been fascinated with the future, especially that of his chosen profession. Because *he* had a copy of Licklider on his shelves, he assumed most everybody else also did. After writing a trilogy of volumes of case studies for public library administrators and practitioners, he, in search of a new vehicle for his literary talents and seeking to put off for just a while longer writing the great American novel, got around to wondering why no new Licklider books had been brought to his attention. He had it in the back of his mind to embark himself upon the treacherous rocks and shoals of such a topic as the future of libraries, but first he wondered what Licklider, whose book-length treatment of the topic was the only one he had seen, had been up to in the twenty-three years or so since that book had first come out. After all, the author, no longer particularly young himself, had been a callow library school student when the Licklider book had first hit the stands. Because so much had happened to him and the library world since that time he assumed there must be enough material for ten books, maybe eleven.

Finding that Wayne State University libraries had no edition of Licklider more recent than 1965, and that the massive main branch of the Detroit Public Library did not even have it, he consulted *Books in Print* to determine what was the most recent edition in print. Imagine his surprise when he learned that it wasn't listed in *BIP* at all! Surely, some error had been made. So he called the publisher in Cambridge, Massachusetts, and asked what the latest edition of the book was. He was told by M.I.T. Press that the book was long since out of print. Why? Well, it hadn't sold all that many copies when it was new and time hadn't increased its relevancy to the profession. Speculation aside, the figures didn't lie: it just wasn't in demand, then or now.

Think of it! The only full-length book on the future of libraries was out of print! Did that say something about the book, or the whole profession? The profession evidently cared little for speculation about its own future, or this book would have been in its sixth revised edition, having sold thousands of copies in its first five. To let this book languish on the publisher's shelves and eventually die an unnoticed death bespeaks a puzzling lack of pride in one's profession and a similar lack of curiosity about where it is going. True, articles on the future of the profession or some subset of it abound in the literature of libraries. But there are no books. The author thus vacillated between a keen sense of outrage and a growing sense of opportunity. Why not update the book himself? Why not write a book about the future of libraries, only rather than emulating the scientific prose of the Licklider study, create a series of scenarios about possible futures for libraries, which the readership would be free to critique, endorse, modify, improve, or rewrite, as suited their feelings, tastes, inclinations, and moods?

At least those were the thoughts of the more optimistic side of his personality. The other half of his brain was clamoring for attention, pointing out that maybe Licklider's book's consignment to the dustbin of professional library literature was not an accident but a deliberate turning away from an inessential and not terribly interesting book. Fair enough. This book may also be judged by libraries and readers as inessential, but it is sincerely hoped that nobody can say it's boring or tedious in its presentation. With that warning, you may begin reading at your own risk. What've you got to lose? After all, it's not as though your professional future is tied up in any of this, is it?

LICKLIDER'S PROCOGNITIVE SYSTEM

So what did Licklider say that made his book so forgettable? Well, actually, it's pretty interesting reading. Licklider's *Libraries of the Future*, the only book-length treatment of the topic which has ever appeared in the United States, speculates about the future of the library by the turn of the century. Licklider foresees a library of the year 2000 as not being a building of bricks and mortar and walls and desks, but rather what he calls a *procognitive* system, which will not only store and retrieve the information and materials wanted by its patrons, but will also provide them in the most convenient manner. His parameters for such a procognitive system are listed below. Wherever possible, Licklider's wording has been preserved. Some condensation and trimming has taken place, however, for brevity's sake.

A procognitive information system, according to Licklider, will be available when and where needed, provide both documents and facts, permit several different types of input and output, facilitate its own further development through learning, converse or negotiate with the user, adjust itself to the level of sophistication of the individual user, and converse and negotiate with other systems. Moreover, such a system would be able to keep track of individual users' interests and needs and record all use, charges, bookkeeping, billing, and payment.

As previously stated, Licklider published *Libraries of the Future* in 1965 as a report of a two-year study (1961-1963, Council on Library Resources) funded by the Ford Foundation and conducted by the firm of Bolt, Beranek and Newman, Inc. It was a study of "the applicability of some of the newer techniques for handling information to what goes at present by the name of library work—i.e., the operations connected with assembling information in recorded form and of organizing and making it available for use."[1]

Licklider points out that mankind has been complaining about the quantity of reading matter and the scarcity of time for reading it at least since Biblical days, and in our own day these complaints have become increasingly numerous and shrill. He credits Vannevar Bush (for further discussion of Bush see chapter 5) with the "article that may be said to have opened the current campaign on the 'information problem' ..." and cites the growth of information and the increasing difficulty we all experience of putting our fingers on just what we need at the moment.[2] Remember, this was a quarter of a century ago.

Research libraries were already then becoming choked from the proliferation of publication, with more stacks and more complicated catalogs. (Today's terminal access to holdings may make it easier or harder to access information.) Licklider's question, essentially the same one posed by this book, is "How should one explore the library of the future?" Bush's speculative article proposed one way. Interestingly, just about everything that Bush proposed for his fanciful "Memex" is today available to computer users and is within the price range of many libraries and even some private citizens.

Licklider's work came just about halfway between Bush (1945) and this study (1988). Twenty years had elapsed between Bush and Licklider. Now twenty-three more years have passed since Licklider's work was published. With normal doubling time of research libraries (approximately twelve years), four times the problem of 1965 is now with us and financial support for libraries has not kept pace. However, at the same time some help and comfort have come about as computers have generally become faster, cheaper, more powerful, more retentive, more accessible, more user friendly, more efficient, and more capable, with the passing years.

Computers existed at the time of Bush's article, but they were few and far between, big, awkward, slow, of limited capabilities, extremely sensitive to changes in atmospheric conditions, expensive, and frequently unreliable. Moreover, they were almost exclusively military in purpose and function. Early computers were such that one didn't walk over to the computer, one walked *into* it. And if one wore nylon hose or the wrong shoes, static electricity could interfere with the workings of the machine. Finally, the machine ran on vacuum tubes, which ran hot and were subject to frequent replacement.

Licklider begins his book by discussing the relevance of the digital computer to the library, circa 1962-1963, when, by today's standards, automation was still in its childhood. He feels the computer is one of the machines which will comprise procognitive systems, a term he prefers to the more sensational "library systems of the future." He searches for schemata from which to construct future systems to facilitate man's interaction with knowledge and information. Procognitive systems, he asserts, are broader than present-day libraries and will "extend farther into the process of generating, organizing and using knowledge" than a library in the early 1960s can.[3] Procognitive systems, intended to promote the advancement and application of knowledge, is the term Licklider uses to refer to "neolibrary" systems.

Technical jargon aside, all Licklider really seems to be saying is that we shouldn't get hung up on the traditional meaning of the terms *book* and *library* and that we should consider only information and the medium for obtaining it, as opposed to the format containing it: walls, shelves, catalog drawers, and desks.

The applicability of digital computers, Licklider says, lies in the following, which contribute to procognitive systems:

1. random-access memory

2. content-addressable memory

3. parallel processing

4. cathode-ray-oscilliscope displays and light pens

5. procedures, subroutines, and related components of computer programs

6. hierarchical and recursive program structures

7. list structures

8. procedure-oriented and problem-oriented languages

9. xerographic output units

10. time-sharing computer systems with remote user stations[4]

Licklider thus envisioned the outlines, if not all the details, of what we have in today's libraries: high-speed computers, ROM disks, modems, online utilities with over 300 databases available, laser printers, the mouse, print shop programs, microcircuitry, and expert systems (artificial intelligence). The aims, requirements, and criteria for procognitive systems (acquisition of knowledge, organization of knowledge, and use of knowledge) really haven't changed through time. Licklider predicts "By the year 2000, information and knowledge may be as important as mobility."[5]

Licklider also believes in the continuing importance of human minds at work in an efficient information system, which is somehow gratifying:

> The user of a procognitive system at a loss can press buttons which ask "Where am I" or "What should I do next?" Through either of these programs, the user can reach a human librarian.[6]

Licklider's optimism about the procognitive system is not shared unanimously by scholars contemplating the future of libraries. Ellsworth Mason, some six years after the publication of Licklider's book, had a different vision of the value of machine-based procognitive systems:

> My observation convinced me that the computer is not for library use; that all promises offered in its name are completely fraudulent; that not only is it extremely expensive compared to other methods at this time, but that it will become increasingly expensive in the future; that it has been wrapped so completely in an aura of unreason that fine intelligences are completely uprooted when talking about it; that its use in a library weakens the library as a whole by drawing off large sums of money for a small return; and that it should be stamped out.[7]

Mason is not alone in this belief. Other respected writers with negative views of automation as the correct and inevitable answer to the problems of libraries of today and tomorrow may be found in the pages of library literature. If there is even a small portion of truth in the writings of Mason, maybe we whose libraries are creeping, sometimes careening, towards mechanization of services ought to take a long, hard look at our present pathways and our anticipated destinations. This author by no means shares the alarm and distaste of Mason for technological libraries and library systems. He is merely asking what if Mason is right? Since Mason published his article in 1971, so many changes have taken place it is fair to say that it is now a different time with a different set of opportunities, players, objectives, and constraints.

The computerization of the library in 1971, when the budding DIALOG information system offered about a dozen files to its subscribers, cannot reasonably be compared with today's information facility, in which DIALOG has passed the 300 mark and is bringing new files onto its system at the rate of three to five per month. It's a whole new ball game, which calls for different perspectives and different ways of viewing the rules, the play of the game, and the means of keeping score.

What all this proves is that (1) speculation about the future has always been with us and always will; (2) today's pipedreams and fantasies are often tomorrow's reality, just as yesterday's fanciful flights have frequently become today's everyday occurrences; (3) the future sometimes comes around a corner you didn't see before and takes you by surprise; and (4) speculation about the future is important. In the latter case, there is the possibility that if you write down your musings, ideas, and proposals and communicate them to others, someone else may read them and may begin to tinker with them, working out the details of what for you was only a fuzzy concept. The author hopes that this in itself justifies the existence of a book of this sort.

> I never think of the future. It comes soon enough.
> —Albert Einstein

WHY BOTHER?

When people say "Why bother to speculate about the future? It will come soon enough, whether we wish it to or not," the reply may be that the price of failing to consider the future is that one will be unready for it when it arrives. Knowing that certain elements of the future can never be anticipated or guaranteed does not diminish the importance of attempting to prepare for it.

This book will, after some discussion of the future and futuring, move on to as practical an approach as possible concerning *how* one may attempt to prepare for an uncertain future of the public library, and ways to *maximize* the likelihood that you won't be in for as many nasty surprises in that future as you would have been had you never given the future much thought. Then, the groundwork laid and the groundrules established, the book will forge fearlessly forward into the realm of public libraries (or whatever they will be called in the future) and what may lie ahead for them. Not surprisingly, alternate scenario construction, a technique created and evolved for futuring in general, seems to work well enough for libraries. However, only history and its perspective will decide.

There is one final significant problem with a book like this: the future won't sit still while you take its portrait. There is time lag in all publication, and by the time this book reaches its intended audience, statements made will be inoperative, prophesies will be rendered obsolete, and anticipated or dreaded events will not have come to pass. In short, anyone who attempts to predict the future is rash and brave, if not shortsighted and stupid.

Begin with defining terms. Start with this book's title. Let's assume that we can all achieve some level of consensus on what a *library* is (although this author would argue that the term should be left deliberately fuzzy, encompassing everything and every agency which performs any function attributed to libraries and information agencies). There remains the delicate question of defining the other signficant term in the title, the *future*, before we can begin to link them (in the Boolean sense) and explore them.

Edward Cornish conceptualizes the term, *The Future*, as having at least five subspecies:

1. The "immediate future" (very soon ... tonight or in the next five weeks or months).

2. The "near-term" future, which is the next one to five years (although there is room for reasonable persons to see a difference between "next year" and "five years from today."

3. The "middle-range" future, five to twenty years from now.

4. The "long-range" future, occurring twenty to fifty years hence.

5. The "far" future, happening fifty years or more from now.[8]

This classification can be used to stake out the realm of this book's scope, which is the far end of the middle-range future, twelve to twenty-five years hence. The years will be, roughly, from 2000 to around 2015. Licklider dealt with the year 2000, which was a comfortable 35 years off. This book will start at Licklider's target year of 2000, and end about fifteen years later.

The future will be shaped by decisions we make today, which may affect events next month or in our grandchildren's lifetime. The future must not be confused with the results of ephemeral decisions like whether to take an umbrella to work because it may storm or whether to order the salade Niçoise or the cheeseburger for lunch.

SOME STATED ASSUMPTIONS

In preparing this book, the author has learned there are many implicit assumptions in speculation of the future. Rather than attempting to state them all explicitly, which may not be possible, the author has condensed the list down to the seven most important ones.

1. The study of the future is a meaningful exercise which may profit the student, the practitioner, and society in general.

2. Both society and libraries *have* a future (they shall not perish from the earth). Otherwise, why bother?

3. The future will not be all *that* radically different from today, despite the onrushing march of technology. It will just be different, mostly a case of old wine in new bottles.

4. We are not utterly powerless in the face of an uncertain and unknowable future, despite the fact that a high degree of precision in futuring or forecasting is impossible. And even if we fail to predict some future event, we have at least given it some thought, which puts us in a better position than our colleagues who reason that the future will take care of itself.

5. Techniques and procedures evolved in other subject disciplines have relevance for libraries and the information profession.

6. What happens today affects (or at least may influence) what will happen tomorrow in any and all subject fields.

7. It is both useful and important to construct utopian (best-case), dystopian (worst-case) and most likely (middle-case) scenarios of the future of any subject or discipline.

UTOPIANS, DYSTOPIANS, AND INCREMENTALISTS

While a case may be made for saying that there is a complete spectrum of opinion regarding the future of society, futurists may be divided roughly into three classes: utopians, dystopians, and incrementalists or gradualists which include "status quo-ers."

Utopians

Nice to have around on rainy Mondays when things look grim, utopians tend to project an almost boundless faith in the goodness and perfectability of people or at least of science. They feel the future just has to improve people's lot, make life easier, and facilitate their efforts to obtain not only survival but pleasure.

> I have seen the future and it works.
> —Lincoln Steffens

> The only limit to our realization of tomorrow will be our doubts of today.
> —Franklin D. Roosevelt

> The chief message of the futurists is that man is not trapped in an absurd fate but that he can and must choose his destiny—a technological assertion of free will.
> —Bertrand de Jouvenal

Dystopians

Mr. or Ms. Doom and Gloom will always be there to ruin your day by pointing out that people are the most senseless, polluting, selfish, careless, and malignant of all creatures. They believe sooner or later some member of the human race will push the wrong button or release the most potent poison, changing our verdant planet into an uninhabited, cold, and filthy globe of rock hurtling through space around an indifferent sun. Sometimes futurists change sides, from utopian to dystopian and back again. The late, great Herman Kahn, once called by his colleagues "Mr. Bad News," switched sides several times, which confounded and irritated a good percentage of his readership.

> I have seen the future and it doesn't work.
> — Robert Fulford

> If you want a picture of the future, imagine a boot stomping on the human face — forever.... And remember that it is forever.
> — George Orwell

> If you keep on saying that things are going to be bad, you have a good chance of being a prophet.
> — Isaac Bashevis Singer

> The Navy taught you to figure out what was least likely to happen, and the worst thing that could, then count on it.
> — William Brinkley

Gradualists, Minimalists, or Incrementalists

These people hedge their bets, managing to keep their reputations as futurists without going too far out on shaky limbs predicting either the best of all possible worlds or the end of the world. Probably the wisest of the breed, they play it safe, usually out of the honest conviction that nobody can predict the future with any precision. They do, however, give it a shot from time to time, usually making low-risk, short-term predictive statements about particular areas of knowledge in which they are presumed to have some expertise.

> In conditions of great uncertainty, people tend to predict the events that they want to happen actually will happen.
> — Roberta Wohlstetter

> The issue is not whether we should devote attention to events that have not yet occurred, but whether we should be conscious of what we are doing and, through that consciousness, try to do it better.
> — Alvin Toffler

> I have seen the future and it is very much like the
> present — only longer.
>
> — Kehlog Albran

OBJECTIVES OF THIS BOOK

Finally, in this book the author wishes to achieve these ends:

1. To discuss the art/skill/techniques of futuring in all of its subtlety
    and subfields, and ways in which techniques have been evolved which
    can assist librarians (the intended primary audience of this book) to
    forecast the future of libraries.

2. To give some history of futuring and some notion that the past, the
    present, and the future are all interrelated. The author's central thesis
    is that just as the past affected the present, so the present affects the
    future.

3. To get specific. To provide for librarians, from among several
    alternatives, a multiple scenario analysis which is a convenient
    methodology whereby they can attempt to get a preliminary handle
    on their own professional futures and those of their profession and
    institutions. Also provided will be suggestions as to how librarians
    may write their own, better, or more specific scenarios of what they
    hope to have happen (or what they wish to prevent) in their own
    libraries.

4. To lay out a series of alternative scenarios for the public library,
    ranging from dystopian to utopian, with several intermediate incre-
    mentalist stops, for librarians to read, discuss, criticize, improve
    upon, and rewrite to their own specifications and conditions. These
    will be alternate specific application scenarios for public libraries.

5. To identify and discuss techniques which futurists considering public
    libraries may use to plan their tomorrows. All these are written for
    the nontechnical, nonquantitative, nonspecialist, like the author,
    who'd never get his checkbook right were it not for the calculator on
    his Macintosh.

> If we do not learn from history, we shall be compelled to
> relive it. True. But if we do not change the future, we
> shall be compelled to endure it. And that could be
> worse.
>
> — Alvin Toffler

In summary, the decisions we make today will have numerous ramifications and results tomorrow. From a career standpoint, this is just as important
for librarians or information professionals as it is for those in the Pentagon
who spend their days trying to figure out Soviet intentions in the Middle East.

Finally, a selected bibliography will conclude the work, providing sources both general and specific whereby librarians may delve further into this inviting yet treacherous game of futuring.

> This is the first age that's paid much attention to the future, which is a little ironic, since we may not have one.
> — Arthur C. Clarke

> The trouble with our time is that the future is not what it used to be.
> — Paul Valéry

This book doesn't come right out and venture to predict *anything*, exactly. Rather, it attempts to suggest alternative possibilities, for public libraries, in scenario form, leaving to the reader the intermediate steps requisite to making something happen or to prevent it from ever happening. This has the advantage of making the author look wise if the things he speculates will come to pass do in fact come to pass, and it covers his *derrière* when they don't. In short, the art of appearing wise, or at least not appearing totally stupid, lies in covering yourself, either way.

> It is the business of the future to be dangerous.
> — Alfred North Whitehead

NOTES

1. J. C. R. Licklider, *Libraries of the Future* (Cambridge, Mass.: The M.I.T. Press, 1965), v.

2. Ibid., v.

3. Ibid., 6.

4. Ibid., 36-38.

5. Ibid., 33.

6. Ibid., 35.

7. Ellsworth Mason, "Along the Academic Way," *Library Journal* 96 (May 15, 1971): 1675.

8. Edward Cornish, *The Study of the Future* (Bethesda, Md.: World Future Society, 1977).

THE DEMON WHICH IS DESTROYING THE PEOPLE

Mechanization: Friend or Foe? Workers have long had mixed feelings about machinery:
On the one hand, they recognized that the machines spared them much back-breaking
labor; on the other, the machines were seen as taking away the workers' jobs. This 1882
cartoon portrays mechanization as a monster, spelling doom for the workers.

Illustration: The Bettman Archive, New York.

2
Who and What Are Futurists?

I did not say that the future could be foretold but I said
that its conditions could be foretold. We should be less
and less bound by the engagements of the past and more
and more ruled by a realization of the creative effect of
our efforts.

—H. G. Wells
The Shape of Things to Come. 1933

The future is such a large field that one hardly knows where to begin in its contemplation and study. First, who is a futurist? You are, for a start. Everyone turns on the radio or television to get the weather forecast so that he or she can better prepare for such a contingency. When you plan, do you make alternate plans in case your primary ones fall through? If you make arrangements for movies, picnics, bowling dates, concerts, football games, television viewing, or lunch with a friend, you're a futurist. Contingency plans ("Well, if it rains, we'll just have to move the whole party inside") are a part of every thinking person's day. So there is nothing particularly strange or novel about futurists or futuring. As Walt Kelly's cartoon 'possum, Pogo, once said (in what has now become a cliché) "We have met the enemy, and he is us!"

> When a distinguished but elderly scientist states that something is possible, he is almost certainly right. When he states that something is impossible, he is very probably wrong.
> —Arthur C. Clarke, "Clarke's Law"

A recent cartoon in the Sunday comics showed a man standing before a large bank of impressive computer equipment saying to a colleague "It has the memory of two million elephants." This sums up the peril of viewing today's or tomorrow's technology with yesterday's eyes.

Futurists are people who study the future for credit, teach it to others, or do it as a professional career. They have been called everything from prophets to idle dreamers to planners. They are everywhere, even in our mirrors.

> Anyone who wishes to cope with the future should travel back in imagination a single lifetime—say to 1900—and ask himself just how much of today's technology would be not merely incredible, but incomprehensible to the keenest scientific brains of that time.
> —Arthur C. Clarke

Europeans typically do not use the term *futurist*, but seem to prefer a term credited to Bertrand de Jouvenel, *futurologist*, defined as a scientist who studies *futuribles*. With the reader's indulgence, this book will employ the use of *futurist* throughout. What do full-time, dues-paying, card-carrying, professional futurists do? They think about the future, usually in clearly defined subject areas of study. Anyone trying to consider the future of more than one subject area or discipline is either a very rash, exceedingly intelligent, or crazy person.

Someone once said, "Concerning prediction, I am 90 percent right, 40 percent of the time." An alternative quotation is, "Frequently wrong, yet never in doubt." Perhaps this is accurate and fair; we win some, we lose some, and some plays go 'round the other end where we can't see them. Futurists don't just think about the future, they also write about the future. The reader is referred to the easily accessible and highly entertaining articles found in *The Futurist*, a periodical which may be obtained through membership in the World Future Society or in most libraries with moderate-sized periodicals collections. This author used articles from the last ten years of *The Futurist* as both inspiration and source material.

Futurists form invisible colleges by exchanging information by telephone, the computer, or the mails. They swap and argue theories and schemes, leading to debate, dispute, and to progress, which is occasionally forward. They attend conferences in person or participate through teleconferencing. Who better than a futurist would understand that it is far easier to push electrons and signals around than it is people, papers, or books? Telecommunications signals don't have to change planes in Atlanta, and teleconferencers needn't pay for nights in faraway hotels.

SOME REPRESENTATIVE FUTURISTS AND THEIR PREDICTIONS

Bacon

Friar Roger Bacon (ca. 1214-1292) imagined optical instruments and mechanically propelled boats and flying machines. These devices were far beyond the existing or even foreseeable technology of the time.

More

Sir Thomas More's *Utopia* was a sixteenth-century apocalyptic vision of the future in which the best earthly state possible, Utopia, was achieved by allowing reason (as represented by philosophers) to counsel and advise government. More mixed prophesy and wishful thinking in his vision, as revealed in his conclusion that there are many utopian features "which it is easier for me to wish for in our states than to have any hope of seeing realized." He has been variously termed the first utopian, the first dystopian (seeing man as an ever-lasting and inseparable blend of good and evil, as a creature of impulses and prejudices as well as mind and reason), and an ultimate realist.

Shipton

Ursula Southiel (Mother) Shipton (1488-1561), a Yorkshire housewife of the sixteenth century, is credited with predicting, in several books of rhymed couplets, the great London fire of 1666, revolution and the rise of Cromwell, a bridge collapse, earthquakes, fires, floods, wars (possibly even the War between the States in America, which didn't even *have* states yet), and the invention of steam power, the telegraph, the railway, the automobile, and the airplane. While her predictions are open to interpretations, they show an uncanny, almost unbelievable knack of foretelling future events. Nobody's perfect, however. She also wrote, "the world to an end shall come/in eighteen hundred and eighty-one."

Nostradamus

Michel de Nostradamus (1503-1566) also employed rhymed couplets, in French and Latin, to foretell the future. Like his contemporary, Shipton, his couplets have been subjected to a variety of interpretations over the centuries. Nonetheless, in the view of many scholars, he is credited with predicting, among many other things, the atomic bombing of Japanese cities, the moon landing, and the abdication of a British king (Edward VIII, later the Duke of Windsor) in favor of his brother. More ominously, Nostradamus foresaw the rise and fall of three tyrants, only two of whom we've already experienced. The description of his first tyrant fits Napoleon closely. The second was to be a dark Aryan from a German-speaking land. Nostradamus named him "Hister" almost four centuries before Adolf Hitler threw most of the world into war. Finally, he predicted an apocalyptic tyrant from a middle eastern land. We can hardly wait.

Cazotte

Jacques Cazotte, a famous French clairvoyant, at a dinner party in Paris in 1788 accurately predicted the deaths of six other guests and the fate of a seventh within six years. He also predicted his own death on the guillotine.

Lincoln

Abraham Lincoln, on several occasions, foresaw the circumstances of his own assassination and funeral through dreams. On election night in 1860, he dreamed that his first term of office would be fruitful, but a terrible event would befall him during his second. In March 1865, one month before his assassination, he dreamed of being informed by a White House guard of his own demise at the hands of a gunman.

Bellamy

Edward Bellamy's novel *Looking Backward*, which he termed a romance, borrows the Rip Van Winkle theme of Washington Irving. He transports a young Bostonian from 1887 to 2000 in a period of profound sleep. When this young man awakens, he discovers that an ostensibly utopian society has eliminated chaos and inequalities. A type of social welfare state has ameliorated most of the problems of 1887, but has created new ones, which is usually the way things work. In this book, Bellamy foresaw both world wars and governmental corruption.

Robertson

In 1898, Morgan Robertson, a New York writer of sea stories, published *The Wreck of the Titan*, a novel about a British luxury liner that sinks after hitting an iceberg in the North Atlantic. Fourteen years later, the Titanic sank after hitting an iceberg in the North Atlantic.

Dixon

American socialite Jeane Dixon was sharing breakfast with friends on November 22, 1963, in Washington, D.C. When asked why she was only picking at her eggs florentine, she replied, "I just can't. I'm too upset. Something dreadful is going to happen to the president today." John F. Kennedy was assassinated in Dallas that day, within hours of her experience.

King

Martin Luther King, Jr., in many of his public speeches and private conversations, made reference to the knowledge that he wouldn't be around to see the realization of his civil rights dreams. He was assassinated in 1968.

Watkins

John Elfreth Watkins, Jr., a journalist, wrote a fascinating article of predictions which he called "What May Happen in the Next Hundred Years" for the *Ladies' Home Journal* in December 1900. Some of his predictions were based on his own ideas and others were described as those of "the wisest and most careful men in our greatest institutions of science and learning." The results are a mixed bag. Some predictions have come true, some have not. A few of Watkins's information-related predictions for the year 2000 are presented, along with the present author's assessments of their realization or potential realization.

- The U.S. population will be 500 million (not even close).
- Delivery of goods and services, including mail, will be furnished to homes by pneumatic tubes (not a bad idea, but it never came to pass).
- Photographs will be telegraphed (telefacsimile and television).
- People will see around the world (television).
- Moving pictures will be heard (the first talkies came out in the late 1920s).
- Telephones will reach around the world (they do).
- Grand opera will be heard in the home (radio).
- Free university education (off-and-on experiment, it's been tried).

The Futurist reports that between 1894 and 1950 the following were predicted to come about by the turn of the twenty-first century:

- Vast apartment complexes housing most of the North American population under huge glass skylights
- Everyday space travel with quick trips to exotic planets
- Nuclear-powered automobiles
- An airplane in every garage
- Personal robots for housework
- Disposable dishes to wash down the drain
- Death rays that could destroy people, vehicles, and structures.

SPECULATIVE FICTION

Some of the most productive futurists are not (and have not been) scientists, but are novelists, cinematographers, and other writers of popular, speculative fiction. That is how Jules Verne and H. G. Wells became so popular as futuristic thinkers: they wrote novels with storylines that speculated about advanced technology. In the early twentieth century, science fiction writers (in periodicals, including so-called "comic books," with titles like *Amazing Stories*, *Science Wonder*, *Super Science Stories*, *Nebula*, *Weird Science*, *Weird Fantasy*, and *Popular Science*) wrote and sometimes illustrated prophetic tales of the brave new world of tomorrow. "Read it today, live it tomorrow" was the motto of one of these publications, and many of the marvels speculated about then are today's commonplace reality. Ray Bradbury's *The Martian Chronicles* about the colonization of another planet shortly after the turn of the twenty-first century stands as a classic probe into a future for mankind which is at once wonderful and terrible.

Winston Churchill, then a member of Britain's parliament, wrote "Fifty Years Hence" for *Popular Mechanics* in the 1930s. He went beyond typical predictions of improved flying machines, television/telephones, and other hardware-based technologies and predicted "startling developments ... just beyond our fingertips in the breeding of human beings and the shaping of human nature." Fifty years later, these have yet to materialize, which may be just as well.

Huxley and Orwell

Gloomy predictions of technology's impact on our species were reflected in Aldous Huxley's *Brave New World* (1932), which presented a nightmarish utopian civilization of the twenty-fifth century, and George Orwell's *1984*, published in 1949. The latter projected a totalitarian regime only one generation into Britain's future. In each, government has taken total control of society through manipulation of a form of the human consciousness. Huxley saw conditioning and programming, from womb to tomb, laced with generous state-supplied doses of narcotics as the eventual means of keeping the workers productive, happy, and calm. Orwell's vision, even more frightening, is of mind and language control through intimidation and propaganda.

1984 is both an attempt to predict coming sociopolitical events and trends and a warning against a dangerous but unlikely series of such events and trends. David Goodman in the December 1978 *The Futurist* said that more than 100 out of 137 predictions about society in 1984 had already come true, but that most of them were technological events rather than social or political ones. Orwell's new world was England in the middle-future in which a totalitarian (based on Stalinist Soviet Union) dictatorship had made freedom, even freedom of thought, first a punishable offense and later a meaningless abstraction. He predicted a manifold increase in government surveillance, so that all personal activity could be spied upon twenty-four hours a day. Winston Smith, Orwell's protagonist, works for the government rewriting current history to suit administrative objectives. Perhaps Orwell's most chilling forecast is the change in language which makes it literally impossible to utter a heretical thought. In the official bureaucratese *newspeak*, the word *free* has little meaning beyond "the dog is free from lice." Orwell's society/government employs electronic surveillance and governmental linguistic manipulation so it is not only extremely dangerous to utter thoughts against the state in words, it is eventually impossible to do so.

An earlier, more sanguine view of the future comes from Le Corbusier, a Swiss architect whose 1922 "City for Three Million" contained widely spaced, modern skyscrapers and underground rail lines and subways. Le Corbusier saw airplanes as the answer to traffic congestion, both as mass transit and as personal vehicles. It is interesting to speculate on what he would have said about today's air traffic congestion. Regarding the automobile, whole generations of Americans grew up reading articles featuring futuristic dream cars, and during World War II one of every three auto dealers expected to sell personal aircraft after the war.

Wells

H. G. Wells, who had written *The Time Machine* and *War of the Worlds* as a young man in the waning years of the nineteenth century, wrote a novel entitled *The Shape of Things to Come* in 1933. It was in this book that he coined the term *atomic bomb* which reflected his heightened pessimism about the way the world was likely to end up:

Certainly nothing could have been more obvious to the people of the early twentieth century than the rapidity with which war was becoming impossible. And as certainly they did not see it. They did not see it until the atomic bombs burst in their fumbling hands.[1]

The physicist Leo Szilard, a Hungarian expatriate living in Berlin, read Wells's novel and determined how a nuclear chain reaction could take place. His theorizing led to the eventual creation of atomic bombs.

Wells is also credited with the invention of time travel and space travel, although the idea was hardly new at his time (compare Cyrano de Bergerac's

Voyages Dans la Lune et le Soleil, 1657-1662). Other predictions by Wells include new weapons, biological and behavior engineering, radio communications, lunar explanation, central heating for homes, and automated kitchens. Wells, once a believer in the eventual perfectability of mankind, turned pessimistic and dystopian late in life. Ill, depressed, and tired, he published *Mind at the End of Its Tether* early in 1945, in which his predictions were culminated with this depressing thought:

> There is no way out or round or through. Our universe is not merely bankrupt; there remains no dividend at all; it has not simply liquidated; it is going clean out of existence, leaving not a wrack behind.[2]

Helmer

In 1967, Olaf Helmer made predictions about the year 2000 which he shrewdly divided into three categories, events he saw as being virtually certain, very likely, and less probable. Only two of his predictions are given here in each category, one in the realm of science, the other in the field which concerns us most — information provision and access:

1. Things virtually certain:

    *   *Science:* The life span of many people will be extended through the common practice of replacing worn or diseased organs by implanting artificial plastic and electronic organs.

    *   *Information:* People will largely live in urban complexes, surrounded by numerous automata. In particular, there will be central data banks and libraries with fully automated access ... highly sophisticated teaching machines will be in wide use, portable video telephones will facilitate communication among persons everywhere, and this process will be further enhanced by the availability of automated translation from one language to another.

2. Things not quite so certain but very probable:

    *   *Science:* It will be possible to control the weather regionally to a large extent.

    *   *Information:* Highly intelligent machines will exist that will act as effective collaborators of scientists and engineers.

3. Things less probable but which still have a good chance of being part of the world of 2000:

    *   *Science:* Our highway transportation may be fully automated.

    *   *Information:* Cooperation between man and machine may have progressed to the point of actual symbiosis, in the sense of enabling man to extend his intelligence by direct electromechanical interaction between his brain and a computing machine.

Futuribles

Bertrand de Jouvenel coined the French term *futurible*, which is defined as an imagined future event which can be projected step by step from the best current knowledge. Some futurists teach the future, preparing students for careers whose precise roles and natures are not totally understood as yet and whose names and duties haven't yet been invented. Sometimes, they even shape the future, making input into collective decisions which affect events yet to take place. People sometimes sneer at futurists for what they see as idle or foolish dreaming, saying that no one can tell what's coming so it's best just to sit back and let it come. Futurists absorb such calumny; some wear it proudly. When the future comes there are three distinct possibilities: (1) everyone will be ready, having anticipated correctly what was to come; (2) no one will be ready, because no one did or could anticipate a development which literally changed the world we live in; or (3) some will be more ready than others for future developments in their chosen fields. In the latter case, those who are prepared will be so not because of clairvoyance or second sight, although that would be helpful, or even because of luck, but primarily because they already have considered the possibility and likelihood of certain events and made at least preliminary attempts to figure out what to do about them.

What futurists are saying to a world sometimes uncaring, sometimes skeptical, and sometimes hostile (remember Dante's inner ring of hell and the severe punishment for attempting to divine the future) is that they do what they do in the attempt to insure that they at least are among the "some" alluded to in number 3 above. As long as *somebody* is clear-sighted enough to lead, there's hope for the rest of us.

FUTURIST METHODOLOGIES THROUGH THE AGES

This brings us to some of the techniques used by futurists to try to do what might seem, at first blush, to be impossible for the overwhelming majority of us who can never predict the winner of the "superfecta" at race-tracks or calculate the winners of all the NFL football games on any given Sunday. The following list includes some of the job titles and devices of those who attempt or have attempted to divine the future: analysis of trends, astrology, astronomers, anticipation, augury, clairvoyants, computer simulation, conjecture, conjurers, contingency planning, cross-impact matrix analysis, crystal balls, decision trees, DELPHI methodology, diviners, dream interpretation, ESP (extrasensory perception), entrails of animals and birds, expectation, factor analysis, forecasting, foresight, fortune-tellers, future circles, futuring, game theory, gaming, guesswork, gut instinct, handicapping, horoscopes, hunches, i ching, intuition, magicians, mystics, narcotic visions, necromancy, occult science, oddsmakers, oracles, omens, palmistry, phrenology, portents, parapsychology, precognition, prediction, premonitions, presaging, probability theory, prognostications, projection, prophecy, prospect analysis, psychics, pythonesses, regression analysis, relevance trees, séances, second sight, seers, sibyls, simulation, sixth sense, sorcery, speculation, spiritualists, statistical analysis, tarot cards, tea leaves, telepathy, trances, trend extrapolation, visions, and weighted forecasting.

Among these six dozen or so methods and techniques, only a few are even remotely scientific in that they can be explained, tested, and repeated. The rest are conjectural at best, based on a mixture of wishful thinking, fears, worries, hopes, dreams, and mystery. All we can say with conviction is that:

1. No one was ever or ever will be perfect in predicting what is to come.

2. The future is infinitely surprising. As Al Jolson is credited with saying in the late 1920s, "Stick around. You ain't seen nothing, yet!" Al would be amazed at what's going on every day, as the 1980s roll into the 1990s.

3. Somehow (no one knows just how or why) some people are better at forecasting and prediction than others. There are experimental subjects who can "tell" which cards are being held up at a rate many times greater than chance would dictate, while most of us would be right every now and again, consistent with the laws of probability. There are documented cases of psychics being able to visit a murder site and describe the murderer and the circumstances of the murder with uncanny accuracy. Nobody has explained these powers, but parapsychology and other branches of modern science are hard at work trying.

WIN SOME, LOSE SOME: SOME FAILED PREDICTIONS

> Democratic nations care but little for what has been, but are haunted by visions of what will be; in this direction, their unbounded imagination grows and dilates beyond all measure.
>
> — Alexis de Tocqueville
> on the American mind, 1830

Not all forecasters are right on the money, or even close. As reported earlier, Mrs. Shipton predicted that the world would end in 1881. Other failed predictions include:

1. At the beginning of the twentieth century, scientists were almost unanimous in declaring that heavier-than-air flight was impossible and that anyone who attempted to build airplanes was a fool. A *New York Times* editorial in 1903 called the prospect of manned flight a waste of time and money because it would take tons of fuel to lift a few people weighing a combined few hundred pounds.

2. Following World War I, a consulting firm advised General Motors to eliminate its Chevrolet division because the car would never be successful.

3. "Whatever happens in Vietnam, I can conceive of nothing except military victory," said Dwight D. Eisenhower in 1967.

4. When Thomas Edison's electric (incandescent) light bulb was first revealed to the world, gas companies were relieved to hear that noted British scientists told a committee of Parliament that Edison's ideas were "good enough for our transatlantic friends, but unworthy of the attention of practical or scientific men."

5. "What can be more palpably absurd than the prospect held out of locomotives traveling twice as fast as stagecoaches?" — *The Quarterly Review*, 1825.

6. "While theoretically and technically television may be feasible, commercially and financially I consider it an impossibility, a development of which we need waste little time dreaming." — Lee de Forest, U.S. inventor and radio pioneer, 1926.

7. "Landing and moving around the moon offers so many serious problems for human beings that it may take science another 200 years to lick them." — *Science Digest* (August 1948). It took twenty-one years for this one to be realized.

8. "Within the memory of this generation, the earth has been girded with iron and steel, and the electric telegraph and the cable have practically annihilated terrestrial space; these modes of communication have come to stay, and they are the ultimate." — *Atlantic Monthly*, 1902. (Reported in: Paul Dickson, *The Future File* [New York: Rawson Associates, 1977], 231).

9. "The World of 1960" was the title of a film shown to audiences at the 1939 New York World's Fair. In it, the populace of cities in 1960 would glide through the air silently in robocopters, leaving traffic and congestion behind. Cities would be domed, with climate-controlled environments.

10. Soon after World War II, top U.S. scientists dismissed and derided the notion of an accurate intercontinental ballistic missile, and as late as 1956, Britain's Astronomer Royal called the prospect of space travel "utter bilge." — *Time*, 1966.

What does all this prove? Merely that prediction and forecasting are risky business, fraught with perils, and never capable of precision. Still, the failure to predict, to go out on a limb, to be visionary and forecast the future, is punishable by being completely unprepared for all that may follow. Therefore, this book will attempt to forecast not necessarily what will happen, but alternative views of what *might* happen.

> The gee-whiz futurists are always wrong because they believe technological innovation travels in a straight line. It doesn't. It weaves and bobs and lurches and sputters.
>
> — John Naisbitt

NOTES

1. H. G. Wells, *The Shape of Things to Come: The Ultimate Revolution* (London: Hutchinson & Co., Ltd., 1933): 148.

2. Ibid., *Mind at the End of Its Tether, and the Happy Turning: A Dream of Life* (New York: Didier, 1946): 46.

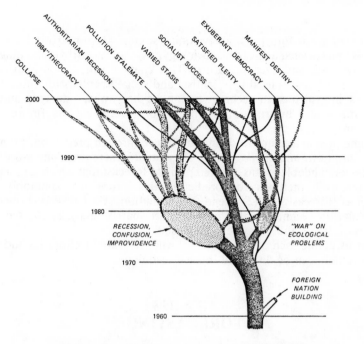

"TREE" OF ALTERNATIVE FUTURE HISTORIES

"Tree" of alternative future histories suggests scenarios of possible developments in the United States during the years ahead. Developed by means of the Field Anomaly Relaxation method, the scenarios are shown as alternative paths extending into the future. Crucial decision points for national policy makers are the "branching" points where one path is selected over another. Once a choice is taken, it may be very difficult or impossible to switch to another, perhaps more desirable branch.

Copyright 1977 by Willis W. Harman. Used with permission.

3
Looking Forward
The Tools of the Futurists

The rule on staying alive as a forecaster is to give 'em a number or give 'em a date, but never give 'em both at once.

— Jane Bryant Quinn

Futurology or futuring is a developing science which borrows freely from other disciplines such as history, sociology, psychology, urban planning, ecological systems, and even literature. This chapter will deal primarily with alternative techniques used by scientists and social scientists for futuring and the ways in which such techniques can be borrowed, adapted, and used by librarians and information scientists for forecasting the future of the profession.

Some people attempt to divine the future through prediction, prognostication, intuition, and clairvoyance. These apart, there are some more legitimate, understandable means of attempting to forecast that which is to happen. Eight scientific methods for predicting the future are commonly used: (1) genius forecasting, (2) trend extrapolation, (3) consensus methods, (4) simulation techniques, (5) cross-impact matrix analysis, (6) scenarios, (7) decision trees, and (8) systems analysis.

Let us define each of these and see what relevance to libraries and information centers can be discerned in each technique.

GENIUS FORECASTING

> Even so imaginative a writer as Jules Verne failed to envisage the speed with which electric technology would produce informational media. He rashly predicted that television would be invented in the 29th century.
> —Marshall McLuhan

This method is used by novelists and writers of science fiction, creators of utopias, etc., who start with the question "what if ..." and go from there. In this way, the individual considers possibilities which are deemed likely or important, acknowledges constraints, adds relevant experience and empirical facts, and comes up with statements of what might occur. The ultimate proof of genius forecasting lies in whether the things predicted eventually come to pass. Science fiction and adventure fall into this category, as Jules Verne's submersible "Nautilus" in *Twenty Thousand Leagues under the Sea* may be seen as the forerunner of today's nuclear submarines. George Orwell also falls in this category with his dystopian *1984*.

> Science fiction is a kind of archaeology of the future.
> —Clifton Fadiman, 1955

TREND EXTRAPOLATION

> In 1960, the average number of occupants per auto-
> mobile passing on the highway was 3.4. By 1980, the
> mean number had shrunk to about 1.6. If present trends
> continue, every third car passing in the year 2000 will be
> *empty!*
>
> — Variously Attributed

Also known as projection, this method involves attempting to extend historical and present patterns and behavior into the future. For example, if the birth rate has risen by 10 percent over each of the past five decades, we may assume that it will rise another 10 percent in the next ten years. Another example for our profession is the concept of collection "doubling time" frequently used by library planners. If every twelve years or so, the bookstock of a library has doubled, we project that another dozen years will bring twice as many books into that library.

Trend extrapolation is risky, however, because it's based on analysis and projection of trends which may not continue. For example, the so-called "baby boom" of the post-war years fizzled in the 1960s. Therefore, the birth rate projected never materialized in those years, for a number of reasons (economic anxiety, working women, fear of nuclear destruction, improved birth control, shifting attitudes towards family size, divorce, etc.). Consequently, some years later school and class size were not as large as anticipated.

Other examples abound. During the Great Society of the mid-1960s, Congress created Title II-B Doctoral Fellowships to provide more and better-prepared professors for library education. The reason behind this legislation was the expected ascendency of information and a concomitant need for librarians to provide it. Well, it didn't exactly happen that way and today a number of library schools have closed their doors, with the total of professorial positions remaining about constant.

Frequently, projection contains a statistical absurdity, yet is logically sound. The automobile passenger example above demonstrates and dramatizes the peril of overreliance on trend extrapolation as a means of divining the future. Extrapolation clearly has its limitations, but should not be neglected as a means of forecasting.

THE CONSENSUS METHOD

> "Futurism" now denotes a growing school of social
> critics, scientists, philosophers, planners, and others
> who concern themselves with the alternatives facing man
> as the human race collides with an onrushing future.
>
> — Alvin Toffler

This method is based on the idea that pooled judgment of informed persons is a relevant measurement of what is to come. This is best typified by the DELPHI method, developed by Olaf Helmer and others in the 1950s, by which a large number of experts in a specific field or discipline are identified and then queried as to both their subjective belief in the likelihood of a specific event taking place by a given year and the desirability of that event. Their anonymous answers are collated and tabulated and then fed back to the experts in a second round. The second time around, the experts are made aware of the judgments of their peers and the percentages of respondents who feel differently. This round usually smoothes out the extreme views and creates more of a consensus than the first round did. Respondents tend to reassess their previous positions in view of the views taken by other participants in this anonymous exercise. After a third round and sometimes even a fourth, which are intended to further refine the process, the results are said to be the shared vision(s) of major participants in the field. This provides guidance for the profession on what to do about trends and likelihoods for the future.

SIMULATION TECHNIQUES

> Perhaps the greatest impulse in trying to foresee and plan the future comes from the combination of having new tools with which to do it and the growing realization that every technological and social innovation has repercussions which spread like a wave through the complex interlocked sections of society.
>
> — Ward Madden

A simulation simplifies and approximates some aspects of reality so it can be surveyed to advantage. It then becomes a dynamic model of a field or profession. A simulation may take the form of a mechanical analog such as the "Flight Simulator" program now in use on microcomputers; a mathematical analog such as a series of equations describing small-group interactions; a metaphorical analog such as using actors, roles, and the stage to stand for persons, relationships, and a setting; and a game such as Monopoly, which simulates competition in the real estate development market. In libraries, games could be devised which explore the consequences of a certain action or changed condition. An example might be the following:

> You are director of a medium-sized public library system in the midwestern United States. Imagine that, subsequent to the death of a prominent local citizen, you are astonished and delighted to learn that he or she has remembered the library in his or her will, providing an unrestricted bequest of $10 million. The only condition is that the money must be entirely spent within a three-month period or unused funds will revert to the estate of the deceased, to be divided among the heirs. What would you do with the money?

Simulation permits you to consider what you would buy and how it might affect the library in the short and long range. Other, usually more austere scenarios for public libraries appear in subsequent chapters of this book.

CROSS-IMPACT MATRIX ANALYSIS

This method takes into account the fact that an event has multiple causes and both intended and unintended effects. This interrelationship between events and developments is called *cross impact*. This technique also reveals probable new problems which are often created when another problem is solved. An example is in the field of medicine, where decreasing infant mortality rates and prolonging life expectancy have created the problems of overpopulation and care of the aging. In a library-related example, the technology of information science and computers have solved or at least decreased many problems of libraries as well as created some layoffs and dismissals as fewer workers were needed to perform the tasks which computers could handle more quickly and efficiently.

Cross-impact matrix analysis sounds technical, and usually is. Computers, however, can be programmed with hundreds of variables to create a simulation of a library. When new stimuli are introduced, all sectors of the simulated library behave according to their functions so that the observer may watch and learn from them. Seeing how fulfillment of each goal impacts and impinges on each other goal is itself an exercise in forecasting. The only catch is that not all ramifications of an action can be foreseen, especially in the long-range (beyond five years) area. This creates an imperfect picture of tomorrow, which is chronic but inevitable.

A computer may also be used to manipulate factors to suggest ways that imagined future events will create changes in the overall operation of the facility. The computer may even show how those changes may produce still other changes, leading to generalizations and inferences.

SCENARIOS

Unlike the astrologers, necromancers, palm-readers, and oracles of the past, today's futurists, for the most part, lay no claim to the ability to predict. Wary of dogmatic statements about what "will" happen, they focus, rather, on the array of alternatives open to decision-makers, stressing that the future is fluid, not fixed or frozen.

—Alvin Toffler

Scenarios, which are the primary vehicle of this book, are narrative descriptions of sequences of events. They may be from past through present to future, from present to future, or totally future, leading to some anticipated future condition(s). Paul Ehrlich and Alvin Toffler are two writers who have speculated about the frequently depressing future of our planet using scenarios with names like "The Great Crash," "Eco-Catastrophe," and even "Eco-Spasm." The eventual truth or falsehood of scenarios, they maintain, is not as important as the exercise of writing them and following them to their logical conclusions. They are fun to write because they permit the use of both imagination and literary talents, and because the more vivid and realistic they are the better.

Scenarios have several advantages as aids to thinking about the future of one's discipline or subject. Specifically, they permit readers to: (1) recognize the future possibilities and consequences of today's actions; (2) dramatize and illustrate the possibilities of those actions; (3) deal with details and dynamics of the real world rather than abstract conditions; (4) understand the interaction of psychological, social, economic, cultural, and political factors, permitting comprehension of several elements at once; (5) consider alternative possible outcomes of real past and present events as well as those contemplated for the future; and (6) use scenarios as artificial case histories where actual real-world examples are lacking.

DECISION TREES

> The United States and the Soviet Union should see what
> kind of a world we want in the year 2000, and, if we
> agree, work back from there.
> —Henry A. Kissinger

A decision tree (see p. 25) is a pictorial representation of the potential results of alternative approaches to crucial decisions. Consider time to be a tree with trunk, and main and subsidiary branches. Each branching is a decision point in time. There are few primary branches and comparatively many secondary ones, so each decision made has an increasing sequence of branching possibilities. Some branches are permitted to grow and branch, while others are trimmed according to the goals of the trimmer. Branches the greatest distance from the ground represent events farthest into the future, while those closest to the ground are those which have just taken place or are just about to. Alternatively, or at the same time, branches to the right of the trunk may represent future events, while events which predate the present may be shown to the left. The bottom of the page, where the trunk is thickest, represents the original intent of the person(s) acting, while upward movement depicts development of events.

For example, consider the public library of today, beset by numerous problems which threaten its existence, both financial and social. What lies ahead, from the standpoint of funding? Specifically, what will the budget of the public library in the United States or Canada be like in the year 2000? A brief list of only six possible futures (from a list whose possibilities approach infinity) would include the following:

1. Status quo: the library continues to be funded at much the same level as it has been.

2. The library receives less funding and economizes because it stops trying to be all things to all people, electing to provide a narrower range of services to everybody.

3. The library receives a lower dollar amount and saves money because it stops trying to be all things to all people and elects to provide a full range of services to only those citizens whose incomes place them below an agreed-upon poverty line.

4. The library ceases to exist as a free, tax-supported civic institution, being forced to adopt one or another scheme modeled on a pay-as-you-go basis.

5. The library receives better funding due to the general perception that it deserves a greater share of the public purse.

6. Something else occurs, changing the library into a different type of institution, with goals quite unlike those of today's public libraries. Examples of these possibilities appear as scenarios in later chapters.

Now imagine a tree with these six possible futures represented as major branches emerging to the right (future) of a main trunk which represents the 1988 typical public library. Each branch will, in turn, branch and branch again as new developments occur to the benefit or detriment of the library. Some branches may actually die or be hacked off and fall to the ground, while others may grow long and luxuriant. These discrete alternative futures are conditions which may emerge from the various responses to decision-point questions. Typical questions might be: What will happen to funding of the public library in the next dozen years? How will user and reader behavior affect library use in those years? and Can the public library continue to exist, given competing financial pressures from other, more critical public services? Decision trees are also called *relevance trees* for obvious reasons. They are intended for deriving alternative short-range futures in a specific field of society.

SYSTEMS ANALYSIS

The crystal ball of prophecy is often clouded, and it is apt to be at its murkiest when man tries to predict what lies in store for him in the fields of science and technology. Prognostication in these areas is a chancy business at best; an invention, a discovery, an improved technique, new materials, can throw the most careful forecast into a cocked hat.

— Roy Brousseau

This is a futures research methodology particularly suited to making public policy decisions. A system is a defined collection of elements with their interconnections considered over a period of time. Once all relevant terms have been defined, the system can be analyzed to see how things change over time. If, for example, we consider a public library as a system, this implies that a collection of elements (components, departments) is somehow interconnected and the functioning of that system is observable over time. The connections may be sociological, psychological, or even economic. It is also possible to intervene in, modify, or veer the system from the decision maker's point of view.

Defining the system is, of course, not easy as it is not always apparent whether elements are inside or outside its boundaries. As an example, interlibrary loan is both a component of the library and a framework imposed from outside the library. Analysis of the system reveals its goals, and change over time may be seen as the measurement of how, and to what extent, the organization is perceived as changing toward or away from its goals.

Goals, however, to be effective, must be commonly agreed upon, and consensus is implied in any systems analysis. Without a clear and consensual statement of what the goals are, how can a library or any other institution ever hope to ascertain whether or not it is reaching or has reached those goals? Techniques of measurement and intervention are similarly in need of careful definition and consensus. Without identification of and agreement upon methods to be used to measure, there can be no agreement on how to pursue goals or whether they have yet been achieved.

Systems analysis is used extensively in educational policy research as a tool for decision makers. A list of potential uses of the techniques involved in systems analysis for public libraries might include:

1. Analysis of basic issues involved in decisions relating to the funding and control of libraries.

2. Descriptions of feasible alternative future library systems and of the policy decisions which would tend to lead toward each.

3. Comparison of alternative means (e.g., funding formulae) for aiming toward a set of goals (financial solvency) for libraries.

4. Analysis of the dynamics of implementing a particular innovation, especially the anticipated interactions among advocates and opponents of the planned change(s).

All of the above futures research methodologies or forecasting skills can provide the library profession with useful clues or probabilities about the future or about possible alternative futures. Still, the unpredictability of the future is patently obvious. Both accidents and the unforeseen consequences of decisions and interventions can radically affect the future in ways which may be startling, surprising, annoying, gratifying, amusing, or horrifying.

> Men occasionally stumble over the truth but most of them pick themselves up and hurry off as if nothing happened.
> — Winston Churchill

Why do forecasts go wrong? Because there are so many variables at play. Keep these in mind when studying the future and futurist's forecasts:

- Unforeseeable historical accidents may occur.

- A forecast may itself lead to or promote decisions and interventions which alter or invalidate the forecast.

- The use of invalid comparisons and analogies between past and future situations may invalidate the forecast.

- Futurists may incorrectly interpret cause-and-effect relationships.

- Futurists may allow their desires or fears to cloud plausibility.

- The investigator may have used unreliable information or lacked pertinent data.

- Futurists may lack imagination and/or courage to persevere or to admit error.

- Incorrect calculations or overcompensation may occur.

- The forecaster may become preoccupied with a single pattern and omit pertinent developments.

This list is by no means exhaustive. Other techniques both old and new are used to anticipate the future. Yet protests are heard in every age condemning the practice of spending large amounts of time, effort, and money trying to figure out what is coming next. It is quite literally impossible to predict the future, yet we must try.

> If a man takes no thought about what is distant, he will
> find sorrow near at hand.
> — Confucius

Our only real choice with respect to the study of the future is between being completely surprised by the future and, therefore, subject to the control of external forces or, alternatively, having some basis of knowledge about what is possible in order to attempt to shape the future in accordance with our own desires and values. To admit that we may not all share the same desires and values does nothing to weaken the case for futuring. Even if we are wrong a good proportion of the time, to study the future is a commitment to freedom. Conversely, to refuse or fail to study the future is to be subject to capricious, indifferent fate. We can only try.

Scenario 1

This is What Happens:

May 1987 Terrorists detonate biochemical bomb
Sep 1989 U.S.S.R. becomes net energy importer
Nov 1989 AIDS is discovered to be spread by mosquitoes
Jan 1990 Childless households increase from 48% to 75%
May 1991 Robot infantrymen are deployed
Jun 1992 Drugs developed to enhance the brain
Apr 1993 U.S. pulls out of Korea
Jan 1994 Learning information network communications
Jan 1994 Earthquake prediction capability is perfected
May 1994 Biochemical warfare in Iraq/Iran war
Dec 1994 New "earth" found at nearby star
Jan 1998 Brain dump to computer is developed
May 1999 Used human parts are reconstituted
Jan 2000 Commission on ethics established
May 2000 Foreign business intelligence center founded
Apr 2001 "Red Tide" devastates Latin economies
Jul 2002 Early warning systems sabotaged
Feb 2003 U.S. no longer number one in farm production
Apr 2006 Global recession

This is What Does NOT Happen:

Engineer/scientist shortage
Polymer-matrix composite materials developed
Mental telepathy validated
Anti-aging drug developed
Brain exams forecast job performance
High unemployment due to no retirement
U.S. pulls out of NATO
Contact with extraterrestrials
Pacific nuclear-free zone
Molecular chip developed
Fission is number-one energy source
Non-nuclear metals memory developed
No restriction on servicewomen
Higher standards in high schools are met

Scenario 2

This is What Happens:

May 1987 U.S.S.R. becomes net energy importer
May 1988 U.S. pulls out of Korea
Oct 1990 Commission on ethics established
Nov 1990 Higher standards in high schools are met
Jun 1991 Molecular chip developed
Oct 1991 U.S. no longer number one in farm production
Jul 1993 Anti-aging drug developed
May 1994 Earthquake prediction capability is perfected
Aug 1994 Fission is number-one energy source
Nov 1994 Learning information network communications
Jan 1996 AIDS is discovered to be spread by mosquitoes
Feb 1996 Childless households increase from 48% to 75%
Oct 1999 No restriction on servicewomen
May 2001 Brain dump to computer is developed
Sep 2004 Terrorists detonate biochemical bomb
Mar 2005 Robot infantrymen are deployed

This is What Does NOT Happen:

Engineer/scientist shortage
Polymer-matrix composite materials developed
Mental telepathy validated
Drugs developed to enhance the brain
Foreign business intelligence center founded
Brain exams forecast job performance
High unemployment due to no retirement
"Red Tide" devastates Latin economies
Early warning systems sabotaged
U.S. pulls out of NATO
Contact with extraterrestrials
New "earth" found at nearby star
Pacific nuclear-free zone
Non-nuclear metals memory developed
Used human parts are reconstituted
Global recession
Biochemical warfare in Iraq/Iran war

This chart shows two alternative scenarios for U.S. national security, based on 33 possible events. SIGMA "rolled the dice" for the events, using probabilities determined by workshop participants, and came up with differing versions of what will or will not occur over the next 20 years.

Futurist William Renfro depicts two alternative futures for the security of the United States. Copyright 1986 by The Policy Analysis Co., Inc. Reprinted with permission.

4

Scenarios and Scenario Building for Libraries of the Future

Bertrand de Jouvenal has suggested that various types of future should be portrayed on TV, allowing the public to vote in a referendum on "the future of your choice." The chief message of the futurists is that man is not trapped in an absurd fate but that he can and must choose his destiny—a technological assertion of free will.

— "The Futurists: Looking toward A.D. 2000"
Time (February 25, 1966): 28-29

Multiple scenario analysis (MSA) is a relatively new approach to introducing uncertainty into the planning process although in a way it is familiar to most of us. For example, athletic teams frequently anticipate the tactics and strategies of upcoming opponents and try out different coping strategies. Military leaders do much the same as American military minds plot, map, and game Soviet intentions in the Middle East, and plan contingency responses to varied ploys and threats. Their counterparts in the Kremlin do much the same thing concerning American intentions.

The word *scenario* is a theatrical term referring to the outline of the plot or a sequence of action in a play or movie. The use of the term in institutional or national planning is generally credited to Herman Kahn, perhaps the most noted of futurists in the mid-1950s. Today the term is in general use by military, strategic, and corporate planners throughout the world. Kahn and Wiener defined scenarios as "hypothetical sequences of events constructed for the purpose of focusing attention on casual processes and decision points."[1] By thinking about the future as multiple scenarios, forecasters deal with ranges of trends and events rather than particular sequences. Scenarios of the future may take many different forms, ranging from a concise outline detailing the range of assumptions to a chapter-length fictionalized essay that reads like a short story such as those in this book. In terms of format, scenarios may be exclusively tabular or exclusively text, or a combination of both.

Hypothetical scenarios illustrate, if not all of the possible options, at least some of the general approaches that may be taken. By comparing one scenario to another, we may, within certain limits, follow them to their logical implications. A good set of scenarios for any given institution or corporate enterprise does the following:

1. It presents a spectrum of possible futures, from no change at all to cataclysmic change, even to the extinction of the institution or enterprise under consideration.

2. It is not exhaustive in scope, but limited to changes the institution can expect if technological, economic, and political conditions and constraints continue.

3. It is comprised of forecasts based on analysis of available data and stated assumptions about the nature and rate of anticipated change.

The purpose of the scenario is to try out an idea for change and follow it through branching and development to its logical conclusion(s).

Alvin Toffler in *The Eco-Spasm Report* considers the global economy from different perspectives, coming up with alternate scenarios for the economic future of the world, ranging from (quite literally) depressing to terrifying: (1) the super-inflation scenario; (2) the generalized depression scenario; and (3) eco-spasm. Finally, he provides what little comfort he can in his dystopian style with a chapter entitled "Coping with Crisis."

I. H. Wilson said, "However good our futures research may be, we shall never be able to escape from the ultimate dilemma that all of our knowledge is about the past, and all of our decisions are about the future."[2] To this, George Will adds, "The future often resembles the past, so a prophet needs a well-stocked memory."[3]

A very useful discussion of scenarios as a futuring tool may be found in Richard B. Heydinger and Rene D. Zentner's "Multiple Scenario Analysis: Introducing Uncertainty into the Planning Process," in *Applying Methods and Techniques of Futures Research*. These authors remind us that nothing is more obvious than the unpredictability of the future. Uncertainty, therefore, is a part of all forecasting and planning. Because of this uncertainty, no planning group can allow itself to rely on a single conception of the future or forecast.

WHY SCENARIOS?

Since no one can predict a future for himself or herself or for an institution with any degree of precision, one way out of the dilemma is to chart a number of alternative possible futures including not only the probable but also the possible. As a result, uncertainty comes to the forefront of planning.

Scenarios provide a context for planning. Alternative projections of reality permit the reader to consider each in terms of its implications for the entity considered. For example, imagine yourself working as an administrator of a public library when the following directive comes down from the powers that be in city government. The city is a fictional midwestern city. It may represent every town or no town.

To: ALL CITY DEPARTMENT HEADS,
         CITY OF RIVERTOWN
From: L. J. LOUGHERY, COMPTROLLER
Subject: ALTERNATE PLANS FOR BUDGET REDUCTION
Date: NOVEMBER 30, 1988

Due to recent events in our community's economic situation, all city departments are hereby requested to submit to my office as soon as possible the following contingency plans for next year's financial planning. We do not, as yet, know the exact scope and degree of our financial shortfall, but we are warned to have plans for austerity management ready as soon as we learn how our annual revenues are affected by recent factory closings and increased welfare rolls. Therefore, we are unavoidably required to ask that each department have the following contingency plans on my desk no later than Monday morning, December 7:

1. Your current budget request for fiscal 1990/91.

2. Your fiscal 1989/90 budget request should a *5 percent* across-the-board reduction in operating expenditures become necessary.

3. Your request should a *10 percent* reduction be needed.

4. Your request should a *15 percent* reduction be needed.

5. Your request should a *20 percent* reduction be needed.

We know that this exercise is both difficult and distasteful, but we are asking you to target services and personnel that you could most do without. The City continues to strive for excellence in all of its public services, and we sincerely hope that such reductions as are indicated in numbers 2-5, above, are not necessary. With the upcoming election and the prevailing mood and circumstances of the people of the community, however, there is little chance of either a local tax increase or more money from the state government in the foreseeable future.

Therefore, you are asked to perform this exercise, being as realistic as possible. Mayor Adams and I, together with the entire city council, most earnestly hope that none of these reductions in service levels will be necessary. Still, contingency plans must be on my desk by the date and time mentioned above. We thank you in advance for your prompt cooperation.

What the fictional comptroller is asking for is alternative scenarios (in this case statistical budget reduction targets) of a short-range future from the library staff and administration to show their readiness for whatever ill wind may blow in from city (or higher levels of) government.

Multiple scenarios communicate to policy makers and funders that although the future is unpredictable, attempts must still be made to anticipate it. A unit's plan is most effective when it can recognize the possibility of any of several distinct scenarios. Edward Cornish, editor of *The Futurist*, states that when we develop a scenario we free ourselves from strict bondage to the past. Unlike trend extrapolation, we are no longer assuming that the future will be consistent with (or exactly like) the past. Multiple scenario analysis is more a technique of judgment and art than of science. Scenarios are more like short stories than complex multiple regression models, which is both their appeal and their major drawback.

SCENARIO DEVELOPMENT

Scenarios (see p. 35), unlike single-point forecasts, not only can encompass probable trends or events but also can include highly improbable yet important developments, as the following diagram will show.

A Simple Typology for Any Future Development

Subjective ⟶ Judgment ↓	Unimportant	Very Important
Highly Likely	Might Consider	Would Definitely Consider
Highly Unlikely	Would Not Consider	Most Likely Would Consider

This simple four-way matrix offers four scenarios. It also illustrates the application of intuition and opinion to relevance judgments or perceptions of the importance of an event. As an example, a library director might consider the death-of-the-library scenario in chapter 6 highly unlikely, but it should nonetheless be considered by anyone charting the course of a library's future. The degree to which administrators believe that the event could happen will determine the subjective amount of consideration accorded to this scenario, amid all the alternative pathways for the library to the year 2000. To make effective use of the diagram, consider the four possible outcomes of this turn of events. Either:

1. The scenario is highly likely to come to pass, yet unimportant.

2. The scenario is highly likely and very important.

3. The scenario is both highly unlikely and unimportant.

4. The scenario is highly unlikely, yet highly important.

Subjecting the death-of-the-library scenario to the four possibilities, we find that number 1 gives us little to worry about since the actual extinction of the library is extremely unlikely, whatever the consequences might be should it happen. Number 2 is something to which we need to accord a great deal of attention since we attach great significance to it *and* see it as almost sure to happen. In the case of number 3, it may be safely shelved with little time for consideration since it isn't very important and it probably won't happen anyway. Number 4 has to do with the realm of wishful thinking, which is either a valid exercise in playing "just suppose" or vacant daydreaming according to the mood and temper of the thinker, since the event, while very desirable, is judged unlikely to occur.

DETERMINATION OF OBJECTIVES AND TIME FRAME

The first step in developing a scenario is to gain clarity about its purposes and time frame. Ask yourself, why am I doing this? Who is it intended to cover? How far into the future do I hope to carry it? A scenario can be used to describe situations that range in scale from all of librarianship to a specific institution or department. The petroleum industry generally employs scenarios with a time frame of ten years, the time required to research, decide, act on, and realize the benefits of a particular strategy (e.g., the extraction of fossil fuels from the ocean floor).

Shorter time frames may be based on the number of years required to plan and execute a specific campaign or to permit change in the enterprise to occur and evolve. In designing scenarios, remember that social and economic forces move slowly, and public attitudes toward change may not manifest themselves immediately. Five to ten years, which seems to be the accepted norm for change to occur, has become the accepted standard for scenarios. This book, rather than using a decade, employs a time span of twenty-five years because adding the additional fifteen years brings one to the target year of 2015.

SELECTION OF ELEMENTS

Scenario development is essentially a process by which elements relevant to the purpose of the scenario are selected from the total environment. In an institution such as a public library, there are so many variables at play that one cannot even hope to control them all. Consequently, the variables we wish to observe and whose changes will most significantly impact the institution as a whole must be selected with deliberation and care. While all variables more or less impinge on human action, scenarios are too limited to embrace all possible variables, and only the most relevant ones can be chosen.

Five principal areas from which elements for scenarios will be chosen can be identified: the social, technological, political, economic, and ecological realms. This holds true for forecasting of alternative futures of nations and states or even for certain industries. For libraries, however, we shall confine ourselves to discussion of three categories:

1. Sociopolitical trends, which affect the environment in which libraries find themselves.

2. Technological trends, in which innovation and modern, automated systems and procedures impact the daily life of libraries.

3. Economic trends, which concern themselves with the funds available within the environment and within the library so that it can carry out its mission and goals.

Clearly these three categories affect one another and, to some degree, interact. A serious cutback of available funds, for example, will retard or curtail the ability of a library to install and utilize automation, while a conservative tide of popular sentiment or elected officials may adversely affect both the economics and technological utilization of libraries.

STATEMENT AND ADOPTION
OF ASSUMPTIONS

Assumptions or fundamental premises, which are conjectures made about how a particular variable will behave in a particular scenario, comprise an important part of creating scenarios. Once its premises are established, the scenario is set. Premises must be made on a thorough understanding of a variable's possible behavior and must be chosen so that a scenario will be informative to its users. Assumptions implicit in this book are listed in its introduction. Without premises, there can be no credibility in findings since any pretense at scientific methodology always begins with stating of assumptions. Ideally, experts and community leaders should be consulted in this and all other stages of futuring so that participants can agree or at least proceed with a knowledge of the assumptions under which the scenarists are working.

METHODS FOR
GENERATING SCENARIOS

Once premises are set, there are two principal methods for generating scenarios, which are sometimes called *hard* and *soft*. Hard methods include mathematics, models, and computers, or encompass cross-impact analysis and computer modeling. The focus in hard methods is on factors that can be quantified such as dollars, budgets, and books. They do not include such variables as value changes or attitudinal shifts. The advantage of hard methods is that they tend to produce methods of rigor and precision. The disadvantage of such methods is that they are not universally present or possible when examining futures for a large and complex institution such as a public library.

Soft methods draw on processes of human judgment, sometimes aided by methods of psychology and sociology. In any case, they do not deal in fact or proof, merely in likelihood and desirability of future events taking place. Scenarios such as those to follow in this book and the DELPHI method fall into this category. Ideally both hard and soft methods should be used whenever possible in scenario development. For this book, however, there is neither the ability nor the facility to develop predictions or projections using hard methods.

Comparison of Characteristics between
Hard and Soft Methodologies

Hard methods are	Soft methods are
Reproducible	Not reproducible
Strictly logical	Intuitive
Sequential	Discontinuous
Quantitative	Descriptive
Data-dependent or mathematical	Not numerical
Constrained by model or analog	Not limited by constraints

PRODUCING SCENARIOS

Bearing in mind the distinction between events and trends, the scenario writer will probably want to use both, for each plays a different role. An event is an expected or unexpected discontinuity. A trend is a course or direction of events, with no precisely defined time limit. A change in trend may follow a certain significant event. To illustrate, when the Dow-Jones average drops over 500 points in one day's trading, as it did in mid-October 1987, that's an event. But when the Dow ends the year a number of points below its close the last trading day of the previous year, that's a trend.

Change is likely to come about as a series of discrete events rather than a trend projected as a smooth curve. This bumpy road to the future calls for alternate scenarios which show what might happen at different decision points so that corrective and remedial action may be taken before it is too late. Acknowledging that there are cause-and-effect relationships between certain events and trends, the glue that holds scenarios together is a mixture of probability and causality, or simply plausibility. Today's trends and conditions will lead to tomorrow's events: conversely, present events will influence future trends.

A format for presenting the scenarios must also be selected. This book uses short stories which read like fiction (see Toffler's *Eco-Spasm Report*). They contain colorful prose and occasionally dialogue. Tabular scenarios also exist, but are not as relevant to the future of public libraries as they are to the petroleum or sugar industries.

WHY USE SCENARIOS?

Multiple scenario analysis is potentially of great use in institutional planning, as it presents alternative futures in circumstances of limited financial resources and takes into account the unpredictability of events. Although detailed treatment of a single future is a possibility, it is shortsighted for libraries to construct plans around a single view of the future. A wise library administration will position their institution for reaction to an unpredictable series of events.

The number of scenarios, which should be decided beforehand, should normally be more than two but less than ten. This book uses eight because the greater the number of elements, the larger the number of scenarios, and the public library has a large number of different elements.

The exercise of wrestling with different scenarios can be a productive means of anticipating the future because they require integrative thinking and an examination of the interplay of many factors. The methodology is neither constraining nor limiting. Human judgment is the most important factor, and the validity of the scenario lies in public acceptance of the judgments expressed by the author. Scenarios also provide a useful context for discussions of planning. "Just suppose that this scenario holds true ..." might be a useful beginning. "Then what?" When each scenario is given a different, catchy title, a useful shared frame of reference has been created for all participants in the planning process.

There are, of course, drawbacks to this method as there are to all others. Trade-off is always present in any decision. Critics point out that time and effort going into scenarios might be better spent in other pursuits. Hastily constructed, internally inconsistent scenarios are not useful or motivating to action and are rarely plausible. Policy makers are of course free to reject all scenarios proposed to them and to attempt their own. That is the beauty of scenario writing: if you don't like the ones you are given, do your own different or better ones, and be prepared to demonstrate and discuss the differences and improvements.

As long as scenario creators begin with a clear understanding of the institution for which they are planning and of that institution's needs, the scenario will do its job and alternative scenarios will present a set of choices. Scenarios will work for libraries as long as we keep them intelligible, useful, interesting, plausible, and relevant to the needs of the institution. In short, paraphrasing Marshall McLuhan, there is no inevitability as long as we are able to think.

NOTES

1. Herman Kahn and A. J. Wiener, *The Year 2000* (New York: Macmillan, 1967).

2. I. H. Wilson, "Sociopolitical Forecasting: A New Dimension to Strategic Planning," *Michigan Business Review* 26 (July 1974): 15.

3. Richard B. Heydinger and Rene D. Zentner, "Multiple Methods and Techniques of Futures Research," in *Applying Methods and Techniques of Futures Research*, ed. James L. Morrison et al. (San Francisco: Jossey-Bass, Inc., 1983), 51-68.

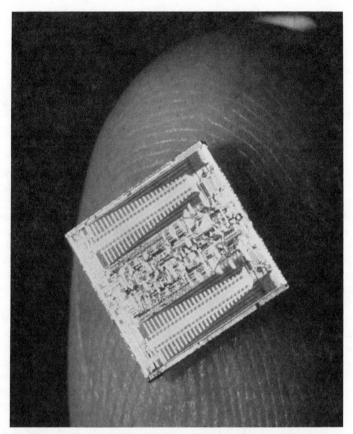

Memory chip resting on a fingertip contains as much electronic logic as once filled an entire room. The reduction in size and cost of microelectronics allows automation of many jobs formerly reserved for human workers.

Photo: IBM. From the February 1981 issue of *The Futurist*. Used with permission.

5
Futuring for Public Libraries

BUSH

J. C. R. Licklider wasn't the first writer who set down his view of what the library or information facility of the future might contain or be. It's generally conceded that it all started over forty years ago with Vannevar Bush. His article entitled "As We May Think," published in the *Atlantic Monthly* in 1945, defined Memex, the ultimate information machine, as:

> a sort of mechanized private file and library.... A memex is a device in which an individual stores all his books, records, and communications, and which is mechanized so that it may be consulted with exceeding speed and flexibility. It is an enlarged intimate supplement to his memory ... it consists of a desk, and while it can presumably be operated from a distance, it is primarily the piece of furniture at which he works. On the top are slanting translucent screens, on which the material can be projected for convenient reading. There is a keyboard, and sets of buttons and levers. Otherwise it looks like an ordinary desk.[1]

Bush envisioned the stored material as being a sort of "improved microfilm," with virtually infinite capability of expansion and storage. Memex also permitted purchase of ready-made contents (on microfilm) ready for insertion. The system could handle books, pictures, current periodicals, newspapers, etc. There was provision for direct entry and a means of entering longhand notes and memoranda. The Memex could be consulted through the usual scheme of indexing, and the person consulting it could follow an indexing trail through coordinate indexing, linking one term or concept with another. New forms of encyclopedias with associative trails running through them would be dropped into the Memex and there amplified.

Bush, writing near the end of a long and depressing global conflict, visualized a brave new world of information storage and retrieval, which would be convenient, rapid, and comprehensive, with information needs of varied types of users considered. Yet, from our current perspective, we realize that what Bush foresaw was little more than a present-day microcomputer with modem, database supplier, telephone connection, and printer.

In 1945, however, Bush no doubt caused many a reader of *Atlantic Monthly* to dismiss his ideas as fanciful and distant in their feasibility, what with a war to finish and postwar reconstruction to plan. Yet today, thanks to the development and improvement of such generally available tools as the microcomputer, the modem, the optical or laser disk, the high-speed printer, and the mouse, everything that Bush envisioned as possible is not only a reality but commonplace, without the cumbersome and slow medium of microform, as he had foretold.

CHILDERS

In September 1971, Tom Childers published a brief article entitled "Community and Library: Some Possible Futures," in which he forecast several alternative futures for the public library, based largely upon his private visions together with his unscientific analysis of trends. What the article lacked in scientific method or statistics, it made up for in being original, interesting and thought provoking for those concerned or entrusted with trying to steer a course for public libraries through the treacherous pathways of the 1970s and 1980s.

The present author intends in subsequent chapters to take Childers's thumbnail sketches of what the library might be like just a few years down the road and to develop each one into a scenario, which will serve as a plausible, fictionalized, projection of practices and trends for the next decade or so. Whereas Childers was writing in 1971, the present author has the advantage of an additional seventeen years of library history and development. Not only will this be an attempt to add detail to the alternatives suggested by Childers, it will put forward other potential directions for the public library which Childers either considered and rejected or didn't consider at all.

Childers subtitled his article "An exploration of the roles which an old institution may find it is playing in a drastically changing world." He correctly states that one cannot begin to determine the kinds of libraries or library services one might wish for until one has made a few guesses or assumptions about the society or community which will exist at that time. Some of Childers's societal or demographic considerations are: population shifts and demographics, usually typified by spreading out, decentralization, and suburbanization; demands for local duplication of urban goals and services; and reliance more on communication than on transportation for information and entertainment. And even though distance will be less and less technically important, there will continue to be, and always will be, a sense of community. He defines *community* as:

> a locality-based social system enduring over time. It consists of networks of interacting individuals and groups occupying a contiguous area for residence who are integrated, to some degree, through sharing common experiences, who have a consciousness of local identity, and separateness from other locality-based social units, and are able to organize and act collectively to meet mutual locality-based problems that may emerge.[2]

This working definition of community seems to hold as true today as it did in 1971, and it probably will serve as long as society continues to exist in a world not ravaged by one of Toffler's nightmarish "spasm" scenarios (see chapter 1). But Childers warns that the term community may be rapidly losing its original meaning due to shifting societal patterns. Children growing up and getting out, going away to college, changing jobs and states, are examples. People now participate in *interest communities*, rather than *place communities*, and form professional *invisible colleges*. These are based on the belief that we have more in common with those who share our work, wherever they live, than with the people just down the hall or across the street who do different work. Electronic telecommunication has accelerated this trend. Costs aside, one may converse with most of the globe's inhabitants simply by knowing the correct telephone or dial-up access number. Of course, costs *cannot* be overlooked; costs are both a variable and a constraint, and have a profound effect on all future planning.

Childers wonders which of several alternative possible futures lies ahead for the public library. Given the changing focus and notion of society, and the ever-present problem of money needed to make library services possible, he asks what future(s) can we predict for the public library? Paraphrasing his ideas, we list some possible futures:

1. The physical library (building) becomes inessential and services are provided directly to people from and in their homes. The library building becomes a museum and cultural monument for the community.

2. Money tightens and, because of other competing, legitimate services, the public library fails in its attempt to keep public funding and slowly (or rapidly) disappears.

3. Libraries continue to exist, for either civic or sentimental reasons, but use falls off to what Childers calls "a trickle of die-hards," as other avenues of getting information and entertainment supplant the library in the public consciousness. After all, in few communities in the world can the public library presently be said to have meaning (use) for over 20 percent of the populace of the community, even where education and interest are common.

4. The library only exists where and when it plays an active social role in the community, taking positions, advocating causes, working for change. However, the community may be resistant (or even hostile) to such a role on the part of the public library.

5. Service to all, a cherished ideal of the public library since its inception, may go the way of the dinosaur. This may lead to revised goals or merely to altered service patterns and philosophies.

6. The library may offer a broader range of services than it currently does. The homogeneous community having disappeared, the homogeneous library will similarly become, perforce, a heterogeneous one, involving a revised mix of personnel, services, and collections. The library will have to provide remedial reading materials at the same time as it does advanced technical subjects.

7. Competition for tax dollars will make the library have to do something prominent, attractive, and important just to survive, before it is curtailed or even abandoned by the public purse in favor of more private ownership and provision of materials.

Today, the wealthy are able to buy many or most of their own reading materials, while the poor find, as always, little time and/or inclination to read as they spend much of their time seeking work, money, and ways of survival. The public library remains a middle-class institution. The middle class, however, feels overwhelmed and unfairly treated by various levels of taxation, and may rebel against having to support the provision of library services through tax dollars. When the police and other crisis-related workers like hospital employees, firefighters, snow-removal employees, and garbage collectors, dramatize their desire for a better wage by going out on strike, the public all too frequently seems willing to give in to their demands. It is better, they figure, to pay such workers what they ask than to have to try and get along without them or their services. But what can libraries (and librarians) do to prevent their slice of the tax-dollar pie from being whittled down to unacceptable levels or eclipsed?

As Childers asks, "How generously will a constituency support an institution that is unused by the majority of adult residents, an institution that may be more a monument than a resource actively responding to the dynamics of society?"[3]

So what can the library do to prevent its own murder, suicide, or enfeeblement? Childers provides some possible alternative futures for the library, any of which could happen but each of which would require consensus, goal-shifting, planning, cooperation, and effective carry-over into a new, usually unfamiliar realm of what we do.

Childers's list was a promising start and a commendable job of trying to carve out a societal niche for the public library before society metaphorically shelves the library in a rundown warehouse on the outskirts of town. But the author contends that the list deserves fleshing out and expansion, and, therefore, has supplied scenarios dealing with the experience parlour, EMP, the library as robot, and "In the Privacy of Your Own Home." Doubtless, there are other viable scenarios, but these will do for a start.

MASON

Turning to our present concern, the public library, consider Marilyn Gell Mason's 1985 speculative essay on the future of the institution. "The Future of the Public Library" contains not scenarios but rather nine forecasts concerning public libraries for about the year 2000. Unlike Childers's alternative visions of reality, these forecasts, all realistic and conservative, are not mutually exclusive ways that the library may insure its survival in about the year 2000. Instead they are predictions about the mid-range future of the public library, specifically the Atlanta-Fulton Public Library, of which she is director. Her predictions, all of which may come true at the same time, include:

1. The public library of the future will be judged not by the size of its collections, but by its success in providing information quickly and accurately.

2. Within ten years over half of the service provided to library users will be to individuals who never come into the library.

3. Public libraries will develop an information infrastructure to provide access to a growing and changing flow of information.

4. This infrastructure will include more, smaller library branches.

5. Levels of service will be developed that will be independent of technology, but will be based instead on staff time required.

6. Fee-based, interactive research services will be developed.

7. A new job title of "Information Specialist" will be introduced into the public library.

8. Book circulation will continue to be an important part of library services.

9. Public libraries will not only survive, they will flourish.

Mason's forecasts are not radical or bold conceptions of what is to come for the public library. In fact, her list is rather conservative. Clearly, she belongs to the incremental or minimalist school of forecasters. Her predictive statements aren't just likely to take place in the next ten years or so, most of her forecasts are already true or about to be realized.

NOTES

1. Vannevar Bush, "As We May Think," *Atlantic Monthly* 176 (July 1945): 101-8.

2. Thomas Childers, "Community and Library: Some Possible Futures," *Library Journal* 96 (September 15, 1971): 2727-30.

3. Ibid., 2728.

The corner video store—now as American as apple pie—wasn't even imaginable 20 years ago. Consumers' demands for such new technologies as video recorders and electronic games are helping to redefine the marketplace and what can be bought or sold in it.

This innocent looking sight may spell doom for the public library as we know it. Photo: C. G. Wagner. From the December 1983 issue of *The Futurist*. Used with permission.

6
The Death of the Library Scenario

October 15, 1992

The administration of the Rivertown Public Library, due to a progressively worsening state and local economy, comes gradually to the realization that the library is in deep financial trouble. This unwelcome news comes during a bleak, quasi-recessionary year at the same time as (or perhaps as a result of) several industrial plant closings in the city and surrounding area. Lillian Harris, the library's director for a dozen years, is informed by the city's budget and planning officer that tax money has quite simply run out for all public services except for the crisis-related services such as police and fire protection, sanitation, public education, welfare, health care programs, and urgent maintenance projects for streets and roads. All other public services, the memo/directive says, are to be evaluated on a case-by-case basis.

Lillian gets on the telephone straightaway, calls the city manager's office, and discovers that decisions made at a recent emergency session of the city council have "zeroed out" tax money for the library effective January 1, 1993. She attempts to protest to Harry McKnight, the young and energetic city manager, but soon realizes that the decision has been made, that he concurs with it, and that it is useless to argue with a city official whose mind is made up. Unwilling just to sit there and take it, however, Lillian requests that an emergency referendum be placed on the ballot during the next election, which will take place in three weeks. McKnight points out that the deadline for filing has long since passed and it is too late to add such a rider to the election ballot. Besides, he explains, although he is sympathetic to the library's plight, he is disinclined to place such a matter on the ballot because his political party is not anxious to be associated with a last-minute tax raiser during a close election. Moreover, McKnight points out, people have their own problems coping with recession and most citizens demonstrably care less for the public library than they do for steady jobs and food on the table. Shaking her head in despair, Lillian goes back to her office to think things over and to plot her next moves.

November 1, 1992

Unable to compete with other, more crisis-oriented public services for a justifiable share of the local tax dollar, unable to attach a referendum rider to the ballot before the electorate, and, finally, unable to get the state government to authorize any bailout funds for the library when the crisis is statewide, Lillian acknowledges defeat to members of her administrative staff. Adding worse news to bad, the library's accounting department, after an all-night session with the computer and its spreadsheet program, figures it can only meet payroll and operating expenses through the end of the calendar year, and even that would entail belt-tightening. The fact that even in better times the library was used by only about 20 percent of its constituents doesn't help matters. Lillian and her staff can think of few economies which would prolong the life of the library more than several days at best and the general atmosphere in the building is funereal. A newspaper campaign is planned to put the library's case before the people citing the "dark ages" which would be occasioned by the closing of the library. Philanthropists, locally and around the state, are solicited for bailout gifts and bequests, but the returns are sparse as the stock market's downturn has investors scared and paper losses for even the area's richest citizens are staggering.

December 4, 1992

The Rivertown Public Library, unable to persuade voters and taxpayers that it is still worth funding at public expense, in spite of spending its last dollars on a media blitz, announces that it must close indefinitely at the start of the new year. Heretofore the library has been nearly 100 percent supported by public money, but now it must either find new sources of revenue to sustain itself or perish in favor of private sector, for-profit information and entertainment providers. Appeals to the community for additional or alternative sources of revenue are of no avail as it's almost Christmastime and depressed families need their money for holiday celebrations.

December 16, 1992

All members of the library staff are informed by registered letters that they are to be furloughed indefinitely, with no promise of immediate recall and little hope for the long-range future. At an emotional staff meeting, the director tells staff members if they are offered work, her best advice is to take it. The annual holiday party is a somber affair this year and the traditional music proclaiming tidings of comfort and joy seems jarringly inappropriate. Some imbibe too much of the eggnog, which is heavily spiked despite the fact it's against city regulations to serve alcoholic beverages. Others sit around glumly, munching holiday treats. Whereas usually the party goes on from closing at 9:00 p.m. to long past midnight, this one's over at a quarter past ten. Lillian and three assistants clean up in silence, but in truth there's little to clean up. People seem to have been excessively neat as though fearful of letting any hint of abandon or festivity pervade the somber atmosphere.

December 31, 1992

The moment no one quite believed would ever arrive is at hand. The library closes at noon. Irving Ross, the massive but stooped custodian who has held the self-awarded title of "chief of security" for 30 years, turns his key in the big front doors for what may be the last time. A few people bid him a happy New Year or goodnight, but Irving can't seem to get any words out and just nods his head, staring out the glass doors at nothing. Ten minutes later, Irving and Lillian are the last to leave. They exit out the staff door, locking it securely behind them. His Adam's apple working furiously, Irving, who has never been in the habit of touching anyone he works with, suddenly hugs Lillian fiercely. After mumbling something into her hair about other chances and better times, he trudges slowly to his car amid a light snowfall. In disbelief and sorrow, Irving turns for one last, lingering look at his second home for three decades before slowly easing himself into his car. Sighing, he drives away down the street, his battered Chevrolet making dark tracks in the light dusting of snow. Lillian departs with a cardboard box of things she may need during the time the library will be closed, which she hopes isn't too long. She hasn't made any appointments for job interviews yet, but she fears that she might need to. "Happy New Year!" she murmurs sarcastically, throwing a mock salute to the now-deserted building. Then she also reflectively begins her long, lonely drive home. She has a big party to go to with her husband, but she'd rather go straight to bed with a good library book and get to sleep long before the stroke of midnight.

January 1-2, 1993

New Year's Day finds the library cold and deserted, which is not unusual for a holiday. What *is* unusual is that on the second of January, a day of brisk winds despite bright sunshine, the Rivertown Public Library does not open for business at 9:00 a.m. for the first Monday since time out of mind. While most people have been well informed through publicity, a few forlorn individuals tug unsuccessfully at the locked front doors and peer inside to glimpse any sign of life or activity. Some notice the hand-lettered sign visible through those doors, which says "The Library Is Closed Pending Further Notice." Then, one at a time, they slowly shuffle off to seek other places to find information or entertainment, or just shelter from the persistent howling wind. After a while, only squirrels from an adjacent oak tree bother to visit the big building on Monroe Street. The rest is silence.

February 5, 1993

Lillian is successful in getting a resolution before a session of the Rivertown City Council which calls for the library to be reopened with at least a skeleton crew. Debate ensues. Lofty ideals are expressed in windy speeches. Arguments include the right to read, the library as an arsenal of a democratic culture, and the generations of children who will never know the pleasures of getting lost in a book. The city council is, however, faced with extremely hard choices for the years ahead or at least until the situation eases. Opponents of the proposal point out that most materials formerly available to citizens through their public library are now available (to those willing to rent or purchase them) through commercial suppliers of books, videocassettes, audiotapes, and the like.

When the question is called, the vote isn't even close. The majority of the council members enact a statute that the library is to remain closed until "things ease up a little," without definition of the expression. Lillian Harris's impassioned plea, although met with expressions of sympathy, still receives a definite "no" vote. Other, more pressing, matters require the attention and the limited resources of the city, and the council moves on to other business. When Lillian arises to leave, few members even look up, although she cannot tell whether they are avoiding her eyes or preoccupied with other matters.

Upon arriving home, Lillian, normally the most good-natured and sweet-tempered of women, deliberately picks up a large yellow ceramic vase, carefully removes its artificial flowers, takes careful aim, and pitches it into the very center of the opposite wall. When it shatters, she feels briefly better. Then she remembers that she and her husband bought that vase twenty-two years ago on their honeymoon and she is more depressed than she was before.

April 23, 1993

The library remains closed. Lillian, who had once been confident that an irate citizenry would march en masse to city hall demanding that their library be restored, now realizes that few actually care. She still receives expressions of outrage and encouragement from the diehard library fans whom she meets on the street but in general the community seems to have absorbed the death of the library with a degree of equanimity. She has heard that video stores are doing land-office business since the library closed and the bookstores are holding their own. It would appear that the private sector has rushed in to fill the vacuum left by the demise of the city's only public information and enlightenment center. Lillian is now working at another job as a stopgap, while she explores the possibility of opening her own information consultancy and search service. It is a dream she has had for a long time, so it seems a golden opportunity. But times are hard and discretionary spending money is scarce and she faces the possibility that she will never be able to make enough money at it to return her investment in time and effort. Moreover, she worries that such a service would cut a large segment of the community completely out of access to information. She might end up giving her services away, which would be humanitarian and noble, but would do nothing to augment the revenue of her own household, which is precarious enough in these difficult times.

May 2, 1993

Lillian drops into the city manager's office ostensibly to see how he is getting along, but actually to remind him that the library is still closed. She receives the unsettling news that an out-of-town developer is interested in the library building as the nucleus of a new shopping center. When Lillian exclaims that the city can't be serious about forgetting about the library forever, Harry McKnight tells her that the city is very serious and if the money is right, so is the developer. "But we have four shopping centers in the area already, and they're all in financial trouble!" she blurts. "Maybe, but this one would be downtown," is McKnight's rejoinder. "One of those new galleria facilities. And we need the tax dollars," he adds. Lillian, whose opinion of human nature has taken a few shocks of late, now realizes that when confronted with a choice of learning and money, most people (and cities) will go for the money every time.

January 1995

Lillian Harris, whose previous position was director of the municipal public library, now works as midwest district manager of a large publishing company. While she still regrets the loss of her job as library director, she is even more depressed about the community's apparent ability to get on with their daily lives without a public library. The fact that other cities have chosen similar routes to survival fails to comfort her. Information needs in the city are now handled by a variety of specialized and general-purpose private-sector information brokers. Also, there is a toll-free library hotline by which private citizens may call the state library and get their questions answered. Entertainment functions are handled capably by private-sector video stores and book-rental stores.

Yes, life goes on in the city, and the library, which once had a shot at being the cultural center of the middle-sized city, now lies defunct. Staff members, for the most part, have found other jobs. A few have moved to the Sunbelt in search of a new, better life. Some swell the unemployment rolls. Others, like Lillian, have found new careers or have gone back to school. The library building opened last month as The Riverfront Galleria, boasting twenty-two shops and restaurants under one roof, a movie theater where the library's auditorium used to be, and a limited amount of free parking in the downtown area.

People have not only accepted the demise of the library, Lillian reflects, but have actually embraced it. The galleria is the trendy, upscale place to lunch for downtown workers and few people seem angry or disturbed about the lack of a public library. Lillian's friends, and even her family members, ask her to come with them to poke around in the boutiques and stores of the new shopping facility. But, she always finds some reason why she doesn't have the time and has thus far refrained from setting foot in the place. Eventually, she will, but not quite yet.

Robotization is proceeding like a juggernaut, driven by soaring labor costs, the plummeting price of high technology, and the increasing intelligence and versatility of robots.

Robot sales clerk: This "shopping machine" utilizes images stored on videodisc and displayed on the top screen and on a videotex screen below. The machine accepts orders and credit-card payments, allowing for a totally electronic sales transaction.

Library uses of robots could trim or abolish the human workforce. Photo: RB Robot Corporation. From the October 1985 issue of *The Futurist*. Used with permission.

Coupling these with inexpensive reproduction of books could replace or severely alter the library's mission and services. Photo: Cableshare Inc. Used with permission.

7
AI

The Library as Robot
(or, The Ballad of John Henry, Round Two)

Now the man who invented that steam drill,
He thought he was mighty fine,
But John Henry drilled down sixteen feet
And the steam drill only made nine, Lord, Lord,
Steam drill only made nine.

And John Henry said to the Cap'n,
Looka yonder what I see,
The hole done choke, the drill done broke,
And you cain't drive steel like me, Lord, Lord,
Cain't drive steel like me.

— *The Ballad of John Henry*

At 9:00 a.m., opening time since the early years of the previous century, the library's doors open to admit the public and reference librarian Pam Frost watches a small crowd of early birds enter the building. At last, the big day is here and the moment of truth is at hand! Overnight, the library's technicians have put the final touches on the system which has been three years in design and execution. The last adjustments have been made, the circuitry has been tested one last time, and the staff is standing by to render assistance. For better or for worse, the Rivertown Public Library is about to unveil ULTISSIMA, its new, automated, intelligent, voice-operated, speaking, ambulatory system to a somewhat skeptical public. Over the past years the library has been remodeled and revamped to accommodate its new style, necessitated by the need to cut staff virtually in half. Now, through two rounds of cuts and attrition, the entire staff has declined from 92 to just under 20 persons. This is a tragedy in human terms, but Pam wonders whether service levels are going to be higher rather than lower because of the changes. Pam is one of the lucky few: her reference job has been preserved. With ULTISSIMA on the job, there just isn't that much need for human reference work, or at least that's the theory. Practice may be another matter.

Partly out of pioneer spirit and partly from the compulsion of dire economic necessity, the Rivertown Public Library is now fully automated and robot equipped, with many public services now handled by artificial intelligence. Experiments and trials are over. Today is for keeps. The ULTISSIMA system control module sits quietly humming to itself behind the circulation counter, prepared to deal with the general public, while small ambulatory utility robots circle the public areas, cleaning the floors and monitoring the light levels. However, they are fully capable of handling routine reference work as well.

Three years in the implementation and it's finally come down to today, the grand reopening of the library. This morning, Pam nervously considers the two vital questions of the day: Is ULTISSIMA ready for the public? And, perhaps more importantly, is the public ready for ULTISSIMA?

Everyone has been assured that ULTISSIMA is capable of handling the work once done by almost a hundred people. Circulation transactions, claiming and overdues, maintenance of all borrower's records, performing a variety of children's programming (including songs, story hours, games, films, and recordings), supporting dozens of remote catalog terminals, and monitoring the temperature and humidity in all library public spaces and stacks are easily handled by its artificial brain. The mobile, robotic part of the system can even perform limited "bouncer" duties, if needed, escorting even the strongest and most belligerent problem patron to the front door with a carefully applied cuff around his arm. Additionally, it can dial the police emergency number in time of trouble; keep and project budget figures on a spreadsheet program; match expressed patron preferences with existing materials; perform selective dissemination of information; update, trace or project circulation figures; tell whether a book or other material is in or out; play the Spanish guitar and the piano; perform acquisitions and billing work; and retrieve and store information quickly and efficiently.

One of the principal benefits to the library, and yet the one which makes Pam most uneasy, is that ULTISSIMA can be run and maintained with a much smaller staff than the more conventional preautomation library system. Moreover, Pam knows the machine never requires breaks, bathroom stops, vacation, annual leave, or sick days. Nor does it goof off like human employees are so prone to do, hiding in the stacks, taking long lunch hours, or discussing recent television programming around the water cooler while they should be carrying on their primary duties. Pam has stopped grieving for those who have lost their jobs in the process, but she remembers clearly that terrible day back in 1998, when two lists appeared on the staff room bulletin board. One was a list of persons who would continue to work for the library and their revised work assignments, while the other listed those who were to be furloughed (that was the word the city used anyway) with one month's severance and a note of appreciation for their understanding.

Here I am, assigned to the task of showing off this machine, this reference robot, when I'd sometimes rather torch it before it gets me too, Pam thinks. When ULTISSIMA learns *my* job, what am I going to do for employment? And they say it does reference work better than people can? No way! There's still no substitute for insight and imagination, and that's something the machine cannot do, whatever else it does. She admits that it is impressive in its ability to converse with the user, but so is she. She refuses to believe that sophisticated programming and a pair of robot arms are any substitute for the creative, associative mind of a trained reference professional.

In more sanguine moments, Pam sees the virtue in using a device that enables her facility to carry out the same or much the same duties with fewer people. ULTISSIMA can do the work of many people, but those people are rendered expendable. The solution to both the information problem and the economic problem is neat, plausible, and cost-effective, she thinks, but wrong nevertheless in human terms. Still, ULTISSIMA is quite a machine, and her library has been blessed, or cursed, with it as a cure for a plethora of woes. Since she cannot change the direction in which the city seems to be headed, Pam decides that she may as well bow to the inevitable and accept it in the hope that the machine is everything it is cracked up to be. At least she still has *her* job, for now.

Reflecting on this, Pam wonders how this marvel of engineering is going to handle reference questions. If there is one area in which she felt proud of her library in the past, it was reference service, in which questions about virtually everything have been handled expeditiously in person, over the telephone, or even by mail. Now ... well, now things are different, and she is curious to see what the system will do with reference questions. She sees no percentage in being anxious, but she is considerably skeptical. Still, she is willing to watch and learn what the public will make of (and do with) the gleaming hunks of metal that are expected to handle all but the most sophisticated reference queries. We shall see, she reflects as the doors open punctually at nine, what we shall see. Turning, she darts nimbly up the stairs to her desk. This should be an interesting day.

It's a wig, Pam says to herself a few minutes later as she watches the woman walk through the doors of the reference department and over to her desk. Pam prides herself on her own appearance and feels that part of that pride is reflected in her powers of observation concerning others. Therefore, she is reasonably certain that the woman who has come to the reference desk wears a wig, although it's hard to tell what the woman really looks like, she is so decked out in heavy makeup surmounted by streaked, ash blonde hair (or wig). Pam does what she's paid to do. "May I help you, ma'am?" she asks, smiling politely.

"Oh, I 'ope so," says the woman in what seems to be a working-class British accent. "Ya see, I've lived 'ere a short time, actually just the fourth house along the street, and I decided I'd best pop roond to the lib'ry to see what it's oop to, what with all the bangin' and clangin' I've 'eard of recent evenings. So, what's all this, then?" she asked, gesturing with one wide-flung arm. "What's it all in aid of?"

Come on, thinks Pam, nobody talks like that! At least not here in Rivertown U.S.A. But Pam is not given to rudeness, and she remembers well her employers' instructions that all library staff, especially now that so many things are new and unfamiliar, are asked to consider themselves to be guides, ambassadors, and sales staff as they introduce the library to the uninitiated. Moreover, she believes in the power and capability of the new expert system on which she has received some (but not much) training, and she welcomes opportunities to test it against the information requirements of the public.

A few days earlier while driving to work, Pam was thinking about ULTISSIMA when an old, not-completely-remembered folksong ran through her mind. She supposed it was from early Americana. Based on legend if not on fact, it concerned a man known as John Henry, a huge, muscular steel-drivin' man, who was respected far and wide for his ability to lay track, dig tunnels, and be otherwise useful in the building of American railroads. Anyway, as near as Pam's memory could reconstruct, one day John Henry received a serious challenge from "the Captain," who had just invented (or maybe borrowed) a "steam drill." This machine was reputed to be able to do everything John Henry (or even a whole gang of John Henrys) could, only faster and without expenditure of human effort, exertion, or sweat. Many verses tell the story of the epic contest between the steam drill and a simple man with a hammer in his hand, to see which can dig the farthest in a specified time period. As Pam recalls, the outcome of the titanic struggle is sort of a draw. The machine chokes on dust and breaks down first, but John Henry subsequently engages in a victory dance of such strenuous hammering that his mighty heart gives out and he lays down his hammer and dies.

The relevance of this old song to her present situation suddenly became so clear to her that Pam, lost in her reverie, just sat at an intersection when the traffic light changed to green. When the furious honking of the driver behind her propelled her on her way, she realized that ULTISSIMA, the thinking machine with robot arms which supposedly can do everything she can, is the city's version of the Captain's steam drill. This casts her and her dwindling number of colleagues in the reference department in the unwelcome role of John Henry, but she is not nearly so anxious to go one-on-one with this machine as John Henry was with his. Besides, John Henry's fate was worse than that of the machine because a busted machine can be fixed.

Pam also realized she was guilty of adversarial thinking. ULTISSIMA is not her enemy. It has no malevolent intentions of cutting her out of a job or reducing her effectiveness. In truth, it has no intentions at all, or so she hopes. Actually, it is an extremely useful tool with the potential for making her life easier, as it contains (and can disgorge on voice command) literally millions of facts, citations, and documents. She is no Luddite, seeking to overthrow innovation by sabotage. She just doesn't want to get fired in favor of some bucket of bolts that doesn't need a paycheck the way she does.

Now she musters a smile for the small woman with the British accent and asks her if she would like a demonstration of the new system, ULTISSIMA. Receiving an affirmative response, she takes the woman over to the nearest of the room's twenty-five bright yellow-and-rose terminals. This one just now sports a flat gray screen in the middle of which is a fancy script log. It says "ULTISSIMA, THE COMPLETE INFORMATION SYSTEM. Press VOICE for input." Guiding the patron to the command position in front of the machine, Pam begins her spiel:

"You see, ma'am, ULTISSIMA responds to voice commands, unlike older systems where you have to type information in to get information out. Just press the button here that says VOICE, and see what happens."

"What d'ye mean, type in information? Huh! Usta be, when I wanted information oot of a lib'ry, alls I 'ad to do was thumb through a card file. By the way, where is the card file, now we mention it? The one what used to be oover there, as I recall?"

"The card catalog? Oh, we got rid of it because we didn't need it any more. ULTISSIMA does its job and more. It's down in the basement just now, but it's eventually bound for the scrap heap. It's been superseded by something much better. Even the computerized catalogs of the eighties, where you had to type in your commands and requests, are going to be replaced by things like this eventually. I'll show you why. Press the purple button that says VOICE. Then watch and listen!"

The woman does as she is told and the screen lights up, going from gray to a light lavender color. Then a voice from within the machine says, in a somewhat mechanical yet clearly female and not unpleasant voice, "GOOD MORNING. MAY I HELP YOU?" The woman starts visibly. " 'Oo said that? Y'mean it talks?" she demands of Pam.

"Go on," says Pam, who is enjoying the experience of introducing the unenlightened to the brave new world of information technology. "Say hello, and ask it something."

Slowly, licking her lips, the woman gives it a try. "Well, yes. Ahh, 'ello, there!" For a few beats nothing happens. The woman's features flit from expectation to disappointment and finally to suspicion. "Oh, I doonno about this," she mutters. "Can you really talk to it and 'ave it talkin' back? I mean, you lot are 'aving a go at me, right? It's a bit o' a joke, like, wif me the pigeon. Any moment now some foonny little man is gonta coom roonin' out 'ere and tell me I'm on the telly, innt he?"

"No, you're not on 'Candid Camera' or whatever you call it back home," Pam laughs. "Speak to it and it speaks right back. It's very conversational. Try again. Only when you're asking it a question, be sure to begin with the word 'Question.'"

"Very well, then," the woman looks resigned to doing her part in a farce. "Ah, helloo!"

"GOOD MORNING," says ULTISSIMA, as it had before, "MAY I HELP YOU?"

"Right. Question: I'd like to know 'oo wrote *Great Expectations*, so may it please you."

In less than a second, the machine intones "GREAT EXPECTATIONS IS THE NAME OF A NOVEL BY DICKENS, CHARLES JOHN HUFFAM. ENGLISH NOVELIST, 1812-1870. DO YOU WISH TO OBTAIN A PRINT COPY OF THE REQUESTED WORK?" Simultaneously, the same words appear on the screen. Visibly shocked, the woman stands there seemingly uncomprehending. Finally, she realizes she has been asked a question and basic courtesy masters her confusion. "Ah, noo, ta. Thanks verra mooch." She looks over at Pam, who whispers, "Ask it something harder now."

She stands a moment in thought. Then she brightens and asks, " 'Oo won the battle of Culloden? One of me ancestors fell there." The screen does not change color and no sound is heard save a small, internal fan in low gear.

"Question! You have to say 'Question,'" Pam prompts.

"Ahh! Verra well, then. Question: When was the battle of Culloden?"

"I CANNOT FIND THE SPECIFIED RECORD. I FIND THE BATTLE OF CULLODEN MOOR, SCOTLAND, APRIL 16, 1746. IS THIS THE SAME OR DIFFERENT?"

"Lord luvva doock!" the old woman exclaims. "What's it want now, then?"

"It's saying that it can't find *exactly* what you ask for, but has found something close. It's telling you that there's no battle of Culloden in its memory bank, but it does have a battle of Culloden Moor and it wonders if you want that information."

"Certainly, I want the bloody information! I just said so, did'n I?"

"Yes. But even though ULTISSIMA may sound or even act like a person, sometimes, it's really just a sophisticated machine. It can't guess. It can only give specific answers to specific questions. Anything you can precisely specify will receive a specific answer."

"Now I get it," said the woman. "All right, Cleverboots," she sneers at the terminal, " 'ere's another one for you then! Question: Is there a God?"

The machine evidently had to think about that one for a while. The seconds tick away, lengthening into a minute. Nothing is said; no words appear on the screen. Finally, as if reluctant to commit itself, the machine says, "THERE IS INSUFFICIENT DATA FOR A REPLY. CAN YOU RESPECIFY?"

"Ahh, never you mind," says the woman, to Pam's disappointment. She would have liked to have seen an answer to that one. Instead the woman asks, "Well, then. Question: How d'ye spell Deuteronomy?" The machine promptly displays the word and its dictionary definition while its voice slowly spells the requested word.

"Verra good. 'Ere's another, then." The woman pauses, thinking hard. "What's the best restaurant in town?"

The voice sounds almost apologetic. "I AM UNABLE TO FURNISH THIS INFORMATION. YOU HAVE ASKED A QUESTION OF OPINION AND EVALUATION. I AM NOT PROGRAMMED TO GIVE OPINIONS. MY LIST OF RESTAURANTS IN RIVERTOWN IS AVAILABLE AS FOLLOWS: (1) ALPHABETICAL, FROM TELEPHONE DIRECTORY; (2) CLASSIFIED, BY TYPE OF FOOD, OR (3) GEOGRAPHICAL, BY REGION OF THE CITY. PLEASE RESPECIFY OR SELECT ONE OF THE ABOVE NUMBERED ITEMS. I CAN ALSO PROVIDE PUBLISHED REVIEWS FROM MAGAZINES AND NEWSPAPER FILES."

The woman and Pam exchanged glances of admiration for both the scope and the diplomacy of the machine. "Question: what's your name?" the woman suddenly exclaims.

"I AM ULTISSIMA, GENERAL PURPOSE INTERACTIVE SYSTEM, VERSION 1, CREATED 1997, MODIFIED 2001. YOU ARE ON TERMINAL 45."

"Question: What's today's date, and what's the weather goonta be tomorrow?"

"TODAY IS MONDAY, FEBRUARY 12, 2001. THE WEATHER FORECAST FOR TOMORROW, ACCORDING TO MY SOURCES, IS CLOUDY AND COLD, HIGH 30, LOW 19 FAHRENHEIT. CELSIUS EQUIVALENCIES ON REQUEST. WINDS MODERATE AND VARIABLE. POSSIBILITY OF SNOW 40 PERCENT TUESDAY, 60 PERCENT WEDNESDAY. A WARMING TREND FOR THE WEEKEND. NOW ASK ME SOMETHING HARD."

"Remarkable!" says the woman softly. "Bloody astonishing!" Pam finds herself nodding in agreement. The machine just seems to sit there, hitting home runs every time and smoothly fielding whatever might come at it, never missing a beat.

The woman steps out of the query position for a moment and winks at Pam, conspiratorially. "Like the races, young lady? Oh, I do! D'ya know, I'm an 'orse player, meself? Learnt to handicap as a girl in England. Lost and won several fortunes by me present age and circumstances. Maybe this machine can be dead useful to me. Let's see." She once again assumes the position of questioner. "Right. Final question, then," she exclaims. " 'Oo's gonta win the first race at Hialeah tomorrow then, eh?"

"THE FIRST RACE TOMORROW, TUESDAY, FEBRUARY 13, 2001, AT THE HIALEAH, FLORIDA, RACETRACK," says ULTISSIMA, "WILL BE A CLAIMING STAKES FOR THREE YEAR OLDS, WITH A $50,000 PURSE. THE TRACK IS EXPECTED TO BE FAST AND CLEAR UNLESS IT RAINS OVERNIGHT. UPON REQUEST, I CAN DISPLAY A TABLE OF ENTRIES AND CURRENT ODDS. REGRETFULLY, I CANNOT PICK WINNERS, HOWEVER. I AM AS YET UNABLE TO SPECULATE ON EVENTS NOT YET TAKING PLACE. PLEASE RESPECIFY YOUR QUESTION."

"I thought as mooch," said the woman, grinning at Pam and turning to leave. "Ahh, well, it's still a grand machine, and that's a fact. Well, knowin' would joost take the foon out of it all, wunnit?" She turns to leave. "Young lady, I've enjoyed meself, and I'll coom back to challenge your fancy machine again. Just now, I've got to get along to the food store, before they sell out of croompets. Tarra!"

Pam isn't too sure what "tarra" means, but she takes it to mean goodbye. " 'Bye, now," she calls after the woman walking slowly away, "come back anytime!" She watches the woman leave the reference department, and turns back to the now-silent ULTISSIMA, whose screen has resumed its original gray, smooth configuration. On an impulse, she stands in the questioner's stance, punches the VOICE button, and after the obligatory "GOOD MORNING, MAY I HELP YOU?" asks softly, "Question: that woman who was just here, was she wearing a wig?"

Two seconds later, the answer comes, spoken softly, almost conspiratorially and, at the same time, across the screen:

"COULD BE. I AM UNABLE TO SPECULATE AND AM NOT PRO-GRAMMED TO ASK OR TOUCH. YOUR GUESS IS AS GOOD AS MINE. PLEASE RESPECIFY."

"Naah, forget it. Thanks." With that, Pam Frost, among the last of Rivertown's reference librarians, walks slowly back to her desk, wondering once again what she is going to do when ULTISSIMA learns a few more tricks.

The traditional library, consisting of books and work tables, may give way to a cultural monument, largely unused but maintained at public expense out of collective guilt. Photo: University of Texas at Austin. From the April 1978 issue of *The Futurist*. Used with permission.

8
The Cultural Monument

Ultimately ... libraries as we know them seem likely to disappear. Facilities will still exist to preserve the print-on-paper record of the past, of course, but they will be more like archives, or even museums, providing little in the way of public service. As for the electronic sources, libraries may have an interim role to play ... to subsidize access to electronic publications.... In the longer term, it seems certain that the library will be bypassed. That is, people will have very little reason to visit libraries in order to gain access to information sources.

—F. W. Lancaster

April 7, 2003

It is a rainy Sunday afternoon and Frank Rossiter, the security guard, is bored out of his mind. After opening the building at noon, as is both usual and statutory, he retreated to the battered and scarred old desk near the automated system to await developments. Very little has happened in the past two hours, which especially on Sundays is par for the course.

About an hour ago, Leroy Smith, an octogenarian pensioner in a well-traveled overcoat, trudged in out of the rain and tipped Frank his customary mock salute. He then shuffled off into the darkened corridors and galleries of the old building which once rang with the voices of hundreds of active library users on any given day, whatever the weather. Leroy is an amateur historian, who seems to have turned his back on the technological triumphs of the twenty-first century, preferring to live (at least in his mind) back in the days when television was a wonder and air-conditioning a rarity. Frank knows how he feels. He has worked for the library for over forty years and for the last few of them, since the turn of the century, he has had little or nothing to do for days at a time. His role was once that of greeter, unofficial information source, patrolman, and, when needed, bouncer. Nowadays, he patrols empty hallways and peers into gloomy, unoccupied rooms. Because all the time on his hands irritates him enormously, Frank spends a lot of time meditating on what went wrong, why the public library became little more than a cultural monument when it once was a contender for the title of cultural and/or intellectual center of the community.

No point in trying to catch a nap, he thinks resignedly. I gotta make rounds in twenty minutes. He sits, nibbling the end of a pencil almost as old as he is, trying to solve a crossword puzzle. Unable to figure out what eight-letter word, beginning with two a's is an "anteater relative," he wonders if the old building contains a dictionary. Haven't seen one of those in years, he realizes although he remembers when the reference area was lined with dictionaries of all types. And there were thousands, maybe millions of other books, and photographs, and movies, and all kinds of other stuff, on all four public floors. Where did they all go? Now, if he could find three hundred books in the whole place, it'd be amazing.

Yeah, he sighs, I was always on my feet in those days, on the prowl. I'd catch people tearing pages out of books, or smoking in the stacks, or fighting, necking, sleeping. Everybody said I had eyes in the back of my head, I was so good at finding out where the bad ones were. Kids up to no good in the stacks! Derelicts sleeping at the index tables. My job was to roust the "undesirable elements" so that the rest could use the building without being bothered. He throws his head back and emits a short, barking laugh which echoes in the empty room. Today, I could throw a grenade into just about any of the rooms upstairs and most days I wouldn't hit nobody! Wouldn't even tear up a lot of books. Just ancient woodwork and dust up there.

Frank spends some time staring out the old, grimy windows of the library's main hall. The rain falls steadily in sheets, tapping lightly against the windowpanes. Frank knows that this weather will mean even fewer Sunday visitors than normal. Fancy that, people don't even use the library to come in out of the rain anymore! One of his few Sunday duties is to write down the tally of people who have come through the turnstiles at the entrance. Over the past six months, the average has been about sixteen. Today, he estimates, we won't get past nine. So far, just predictable old Leroy and an elderly lady are all he has seen, less than one an hour.

Speaking of Leroy, here he comes now. Leroy is a short black man with a full head of curly white hair and a moustache to match. His rimless glasses give him a gentle, scholarly appearance, perfectly suited to his quiet demeanor. Despite his jacket's worn, slightly grubby sleeves, Leroy is a man of dignity and infectious good cheer, and Frank has come to look forward to his conversational visits. Any distraction helps pass the time, he concedes, but Leroy is the highlight of a boring shift. He is in the library most days, whatever the weather, but Sundays are special because so few other people are around. He pores over volumes of world history from the dwindling collection, but he also relishes good conversation.

"Hey, there, Frankie. How you be, today?" he asks, breaking into a sunny, if snaggletoothed smile.

"All right, 'Roy. Can't complain. How's yourself?"

"Quiet in here today, ain't it? I mean, quieter than usual."

"Yeah, nothin' like an all-day rain to keep folks home in their nests. Just you and one old lady since twelve o'clock come in here. But you been comin' in here every Sunday since … since I dunno when. Tell me, when was the last time you saw a crowd in this building?"

"There was that big ol' fire, musta been in '98 or '99, maybe. That brought folks 'round, didn't it?"

"Sure did. Only noisy Sunday since the century began. Four-alarm blaze started in some old books or somethin'. Time the fire was out and the trucks left, there was damage from water, smoke, flames, and the big axes them firemen carry. Those guys love to smash down doors, don't they? Sometimes on rainy days like this, I can still smell that burned paper all through the building. Ruined about two rooms fulla books, that fire did. O'course, that was back when people cared about library books. Times have gotten worse since then."

"Y'know, Frank," says Leroy, sharing an unaccustomed bit of personal information, "I'm eighty-three years old as of last Wednesday. Don't have much goin' for me. Not much to look forward to. Only thing I really enjoy doin', especially when it gets down the end of the month and the money is tight, is comin' to this library. I love books and readin' and talkin' to you an' anybody else wants to have a chat. This place has always been a comfort to me. Never changes, is why. It's always here. Plenty to read, free restrooms, and nobody to bother me 'cept when I want to be bothered. Darn near perfect place for a guy like me. What I want to know is, am I the only one? Why don't other people love this ol' place?"

Frank chuckles softly. "Naw, man, you're not alone. I work here about fifty hours a week, if you can call what I do workin'. Must be a couple hundred folks visit this buildin' on a good week."

Leroy makes a derisive sound. "Couple hundred! Shoot, I 'member when I'd have to fight a couple hundred folks just to get to the card catalog or the men's room, some days."

"Well, that was then and now is now," intones Frank with unassailable logic. Both men survey the vast, empty hall with its marble walls, staircases once majestic and now stained, and huge, lighted globe of the Earth turning 'round and 'round with a faint, mechanical whir. "Now, it may seem stupid, but my contract says that I gotta make rounds of the buildin' every two hours. So I gotta start on patrol now. You wanna come along, 'Roy?"

"Might as well. Tired of sittin'. You'll walk slow up them steps, won't ya Frank?" Frank nods sympathetically and they start off up the grand staircase. "Whatever happened to that information stamps program the fed'ral gummint concocted ten, fifteen years back?" Leroy asks. "I 'member that the feds sent me a letter, tellin' me I was eligible for free information 'cause of my in-di-gent economic status, or some such language, while all them rich folks was havin' to pay for it. An' all I hadda do was wait 'til the mail brung me a package every month with stamps in it. Then I could cash 'em in at the library same as money for answers to questions and like that. Couldn't use 'em for groceries like food stamps, but they had some value for me. Used to trade cigarettes for 'em with some other guys'd rather smoke than read." Leroy's breath is growing severely labored now and Frank, some fifteen years younger, stops halfway up the stairs to let the older man catch his breath.

"Yeah, I 'member information stamps all right. Another example of bureaucratic tomfoolery. Came and went in the same year as I remember. Nobody used 'em, nobody wanted 'em. Then libraries stopped being important, what with a hundred channels on the vids and all the other information and entertainment providers in town, and people used them stamps for fuel or insulation, and not much else." He ponders, scratching his chin. "Fact is, nobody even wanted to steal 'em! That's how valuable they were."

"I heard that!" cackles Leroy. "People said, 'Give me a hundred different channels to watch at home and it's later for the library!'"

"Hey, just be glad you still have a library to come to, man," Frank reminds him. "I remember when city after city decided to trash their libraries. Sold off the books and carted the shelving away. Buildin's turned into museums or movie theaters or fulla them cutesy shops. Whatta they call them? Boutiques, I think. At least we still got a library to sit in when it rains, right? An' I get regular paychecks, an' you get to drag your tired ol' bones in here and catch up on your readin'."

Leroy concedes the point, but mutters as an afterthought, "Big deal!" Then he raises his head thoughtfully. "But what about the kids, Frank? Ain't the city still supposed to do somethin' for kids?"

"In a way, it does," Frank responds. "The city just sort of steps aside and lets the free market operate. Within ten, fifteen blocks of this buildin' in any direction, you can find six or seven places for kids, to give them some entertainment, supervision, and, maybe, culture, after school. And don't forget that all them television channels ain't for watchin' the vids. Kids learn somethin' watching some of 'em. But they don't want to come in here after library books when they can watch a hunnerd channels of full-spectrum entertainment in the comfort of their own living rooms while they're gnawin' on cookies, do they?"

"Naw, s'pose not," says Leroy. He adds something else, but Frank, not listening any longer, has stopped to reflect. "Y'know," he muses, slowly, "usta be eighty, ninety people workin' in here every day and that staff lounge on the ground floor was fulla laughin', talkin' people. Now we got that hunk a junk called a supercomputer down on the main floor an' it controls everythin' practically. Only nine of us left on the staff and not that much for them to do at that. Why they haven't replaced *me* with one of them security robots by now, I can't figure out! The city'd probably have to spend too much money to buy one, although they'd get it back out of my puny salary in a couple of years."

Around them, the huge, empty rooms of the library are in shadows and the only sound they can hear is the wind and the rain on the windows. Leroy tells Frank that he's off to find something good to read for an hour and he'll catch up with him later. After watching the older man shuffle off down the dimly lighted corridor, Frank continues his rounds alone. As he reaches the back stairway, he is surprised to hear the sound of voices and footsteps growing closer. Idly scratching his thinly bladed scalp, he resolves to counter the boredom of the rest of the afternoon by shadowing these people, whomever they might be. Maybe they'll feel like a little conversation. The worst part of this job, Frank realizes, is that there are very few opportunities for good conversation.

Acting on his impulse, Frank follows a father and his son of about ten up the stairs to the fourth floor. As he watches unobtrusively from the shadows, Frank eavesdrops on a conversation:

Father: "See that, Mikey, my boy? That case has books in it like the ones I used to read one after another when I was your age."

Mikey: "Oh, uh, yeah."

Father: "On rainy, dark, nasty days, I'd curl up on the bed in my room with a good book, or maybe two books, a sack of chips, one of cookies, something to drink, and a good reading light and nobody downstairs would see me until dinnertime. Sometimes, I'd even read through dinner."

Mikey: "Reading, huh? Is that because there weren't any multichannel vids yet?"

Father: "No. It was because I loved to read. (pause) I wish you loved to read, kid. You don't know what you're missing."

Mikey: "Hey, Dad, did you say we were going to go get a pizza, or what?"

Father: "Later. But seriously, if you'd like it, I'll take you to some of the used bookstores they still have out on the west side and we'll see if we can buy a couple of adventure books. You'd like that, wouldn't you?"

Mikey: "Dad, please! Get off my case! I know how to read, okay? But don't get started on that book stuff, huh? Nobody I know messes with books anymore. Reading is just too slow moving. If you want to make me happy, get me some holographics or some vid programming, not dumb old books."

Father: "I've got an idea! Why don't I read to you for an hour or so each evening? Like, right after dinner, before the good vids come on. It's something we could do together and you'd quickly discover the fun of books that way."

Mikey: "Ahh, maybe. I don't know. Lemme think about it. See, Dad, my time is pretty structured these days. Homework, you know, and whatever time I've got left I like to spend playing ball or watching the vids. Now about that pizza? I'm hungry."

As Frank watches, both father and son sigh and walk down the corridor. Each one's body language indicates he is unhappy with the other. Frank pauses by the window, watching individual raindrops move at different paces down the pane. He remembers that he enjoyed books when he was a boy. Later, his children had never seemed to have time to read and his grandchildren, now entering their teens, never mention, or have, books at all. "Probably Mikey couldn't figure out how to plug it in if he did get one," Frank says to himself, producing a grating chuckle and a brief coughing fit from his leathery lungs. In another twenty years, books will either have disappeared from the world or they'll be back in vogue, he guesses. Trends are cyclic. Wondering which way the world will turn next has sustained Frank through his sixty-seven years of life. Maybe the only reason he's sticking around is to see what is coming next! His heels echo in the gloomy corridors which once, on rainy Sundays like this one, held hundreds of people, hurrying around the library. Fearful of carrying his depressed state home to his wife, Frank forces himself to think of other things. There's something good on the vids tonight, some interactive holographic show from France. Sensing the irony in his thought, he rasps out a chuckle and continues strolling down lines of cases of book displays, looking idly right and left. His laughter rebounds off the vaulted ceiling and falls mockingly on his own ears.

> The great task of libraries, worldwide, is the preservation of the ordinary.
>
> — *Slow Fires*
> (film on the Preservation of the Human Record)
> Council on Library Resources and the
> Library of Congress, 1987

Form **1040** Department of the Treasury—Internal Revenue Service **2007** (99)
U.S. Individual Income Tax Return

For the year Jan.–Dec. 31, 1988, or other tax year beginning ____, 1988, ending ____, 19 ____ | OMB No. 1545-0074

Label
Use IRS label.
Otherwise,
please print or
type.

Your first name and initial (if joint return, also give spouse's name and initial) | Last name | Your social security number

Present home address (number, street, and apt. no. or rural route). (If a P.O. Box, see page 6 of instructions.) | Spouse's social security number

City, town or post office, state, and ZIP code

For Privacy Act and Paperwork Reduction Act Notice, see Instructions.

Presidential Election Campaign
Do you want $1 to go to this fund? . . . . Yes ☐ No ☐
If joint return, does your spouse want $1 to go to this fund? . Yes ☐ No ☐

Note: Checking "Yes" will not change your tax or reduce your refund.

Filing Status
Check only one box.

1 Single
2 Married filing joint return (even if only one had income)
3 Married filing separate return. Enter spouse's social security no. above and full name here.
4 Head of household (with qualifying person). (See page 7 of instructions.) If the qualifying person is your child but not your dependent, enter child's name here.
5 Qualifying widow(er) with dependent child (year spouse died ▶ 19). (See page 7 of instructions.)

Exemptions
(See Instructions on page 8.)

6a ☐ Yourself If someone (such as your parent) can claim you as a dependent, do not check box 6a.
But be sure to check the box on line 33b on page 2. . . . .
b ☐ Spouse . . . .

No. of boxes checked on 6a and 6b ____

c Dependents:
(1) Name (first, initial, and last name) | (2) Check if under age 5 | (3) If age 5 or older, dependent's social security number | (4) Relationship | (5) No. of months lived in your home in 1988

No. of your children on 6c who:
● lived with you
● didn't live with you due to divorce or separation
No. of other dependents listed on 6c

If more than 6 dependents, see Instructions on page 8.

d If your child didn't live with you but is claimed as your dependent under a pre-1985 agreement, check here . ▶ ☐
e Total number of exemptions claimed . . . .

Add numbers entered on lines above ▶ ☐

Income
Please attach Copy B of your Forms W-2, W-2G, and W-2P here.
If you do not have a W-2, see page 6 of Instructions.

Please attach check or money order here.

7 Wages, salaries, tips, etc. (attach Form(s) W-2) . . . . | 7
8a Taxable interest income (also attach Schedule B if over $400) . . . | 8a
b Tax-exempt interest income (see page 11). DON'T include on line 8a | 8b
9 Dividend income (also attach Schedule B if over $400) . . . . . . | 9
10 Taxable refunds of state and local income taxes, if any, from worksheet on page 11 of Instructions . | 10
11 Alimony received . . . . | 11
12 Business income or (loss) (attach Schedule C) . . . . | 12
13 Capital gain or (loss) (attach Schedule D) . . . . | 13
14 Capital gain distributions not reported on line 13 (see page 11) . . . | 14
15 Other gains or (losses) (attach Form 4797) . . . . | 15
16a Total IRA distributions . . | 16a | 16b Taxable amount (see page 11) | 16b
17a Total pensions and annuities | 17a | 17b Taxable amount (see page 12) | 17b
18 Rents, royalties, partnerships, estates, trusts, etc. (attach Schedule E) . | 18
19 Farm income or (loss) (attach Schedule F) . . . . | 19
20 Unemployment compensation (insurance) (see page 13) . . . . . | 20
21a Social security benefits (see page 13) . . . . | 21a
b Taxable amount, if any, from the worksheet on page 13 . . . . . | 21b
22 Other income (list type and amount—see page 13) . . . . | 22
23 Add the amounts shown in the far right column for lines 7 through 22. This is your **total income** . ▶ | 23

Adjustments to Income
(See Instructions on page 13.)

24 Reimbursed employee business expenses from Form 2106, line 13. | 24
25a Your IRA deduction, from applicable worksheet on page 14 or 15 | 25a
b Spouse's IRA deduction, from applicable worksheet on page 14 or 15 | 25b
26 Self-employed health insurance deduction, from worksheet on page 15 . | 26
27 Keogh retirement plan and self-employed SEP deduction . . . | 27
28 Penalty on early withdrawal of savings . . . . | 28
29 Alimony paid (recipient's last name ____ and social security no. ____) | 29
30 Add lines 24 through 29. These are your **total adjustments** . . . ▶ | 30

Adjusted Gross Income

31 Subtract line 30 from line 23. This is your **adjusted gross income**. If this line is less than $18,576 and a child lived with you, see "Earned Income Credit" (line 56) on page 19 of the Instructions. If you want IRS to figure your tax, see page 16 of the Instructions . . . ▶ | 31

This year's tax form may be next year's library admission card in the 21st century.

9

Social Experimentation

Everything to Some; Some Things to All

This is my prediction for the future—whatever hasn't happened will happen, and no one will be safe from it.

—J. B. S. Haldane

EVERYTHING TO SOME

The rumpled, middle-aged man trudges through the airdoor and into the library building. He stops before a turnstile and a large, gleaming wooden transaction desk. Behind it is a young man, seemingly in his late teens, whose insouciant and cheerful demeanor does a bit to offset the forbidding sign over his head. The sign reads:

WELCOME TO THE RIVERTOWN PUBLIC LIBRARY
ALL PATRONS STOP HERE FOR CLASSIFICATION
AND ADMISSION PROCEDURES.

Russell has just returned to his hometown after a four-year stint with an engineering firm which is conducting mining operations on Mars. Until just now it has felt very good to be home, walking the chilly but familiar streets of an American town again. Even though the heavier gravity of Earth and its moisture-saturated atmosphere have caused his breathing to be somewhat labored, he knows that this sensation is temporary and goes with the territory of interplanetary moving around. Russ is enjoying hearing birds and seeing trees again, even though the day is almost as cold as any he experienced in four years on Mars.

He'd come to the public library where he spent much of his time during his formative years to do a little research on economics. But he had forgotten how much four years can change and stops silently before the sign for a moment seemingly ignoring the clerk.

The young man looks up pleasantly. "Help you, buddy?" He is wearing a badge that says "Artie."

"Um, yes," Russ says. "I've been away for four years and I wanted to come here today and do some research. But even though I grew up using this building and the outside looks about the same, I don't recognize anything at all in here. What does this sign mean? What's this about classification and admission procedures?"

"First off, why don't you tell me what you've come here to find," says Artie. "Then I can tell you whether you're in the right place."

"The right place? Certainly, I'm in the right place. This is the public library, isn't it?"

"Well, yes and no. Depends on how you use the term. Four years can change a lot, I guess you know. Now what brings you in here today?"

Russ hasn't planned to explain to some minor functionary the nature of his mission, but he does it anyway. "Okay, I need to get some figures that compare Soviet and American contributions to the joint exploratory expedition for mining of bauxite and chromium on Mars."

"Buddy, you lucked out," says the young man with an infectious grin. "Your question is economic, that's plain enough. So it's one that this library can answer for you. Lots of other subjects, you'd have to go someplace else."

Russ shakes his head in confusion. Artie is right. Four years have changed a lot. While he's pondering this, the clerk says, "Let's have a look at your ID, so we can get you classified." He holds out his hand expectantly. For a moment, Russ is confused. What ID? Then he remembers the card he was given when he left the space station debriefing room in Chicago, before he was shuttled home to Rivertown. He fishes the card out and hands it to the man. "Why do I have to show this card? Just to get in?"

"Something like that. The card establishes your entry code and cost," says Artie as though explaining something to a small child.

"What do you mean, entry code?"

"Sheesh! All these questions! Where you been hiding for the past four years? Maybe they don't have a system like this on Mars, but don't they have newspapers?"

"I've been driving between dusty cities on Mars or hundreds of meters down in the canals, I guess. Don't see too many newspapers up there. Don't have time to read 'em when I do. Sorry, I guess, I'm out of touch with things today. Can you explain it to me?"

"Ahh, why not? It's a slow morning and I got the time. Well, when you got back to Earth, they gave you this card, didn't they? Okay, let's feed it into the old scanner and see what develops. Then we'll know whether you're in free or you hafta pay, and, if so, how much." The scanner beeps and displays some information on a small screen visible to both Russ and Artie. They both examine the readout.

Only then does Russ notice the second large sign. This one, on the wall behind the clerk's transaction desk, reads:

FEE STRUCTURE

Rivertown Public Library ... Current Prices, Based on Income Level

Poverty Level for February ...... 4026 credits a month *

Total Family Income, per capita, monthly	Percentage of population	Admission fee (daily)**
0.0 - 1.0 poverty level	12 %	none
1.01 to 2.0 poverty level	23 %	20 credits
2.01 to 3.0 poverty level	52 %	45 credits
over 3.0 poverty level	13 %	80 credits

** discount rates available for week, month, year

* determined 1 February 2005 by U.S. Department of Welfare

"Well, your ID shows that you earn big credits. Plenty in the bank, eh?" Russ resents the indignity of having to discuss his finances with a clerk, but he restrains himself from saying anything about it. After all, the object of this exercise is to get past this idiot and into the building. So he stands mute and confines himself to a single grimace of condescending disapproval.

Artie continues, "Your card is coded to show that you're in the top bracket. That means that you gotta pay the full fee, which goes up and down every month according to the tax base, as registered by the city's central computer. In today's case, that comes to, lemme see here, yeah. You want to get into the library? It's gonna debit your account 80 credits. Or you could have a weekly pass for 300, a monthly one for just 1000, or an annual membership for 9000 credits. So, what'll it be?"

Russ is stunned by what he is hearing. "But how did it get like this?" he stammers lamely.

Artie's smile grows even broader. Obviously, he enjoys talking about the changes the library has undergone in the past several years. He settles more comfortably into his chair to declaim, "Listen, I'm no economist. I just work here at this library desk. Next year, they'll probably replace me with a robot. Happening all over, in other cities. Maybe we're next. Think I'm not worried? I'm worried plenty about what I'm going to be doing then, lemme tell ya. But I read things and hear things, ya know? So here's what I've gathered from all that's happened around here in the past ten years or so. You got a little time to hear all this?"

"It looks as though I do, yes," responds Russ, who is now more curious than offended.

"So, sometime in the early 1990s, the people who chart the course of public libraries figured out that they were going quickly broke as publicly supported institutions and they had to do something to stay alive, otherwise they'd be history. And you better believe that there were plenty other places, like about eight bookstores, dozens of videostores, and the like, who were ready to pick up the slack if the public library just sorta folded up its operation."

"The way I get it, public libraries realized, maybe too late, that they couldn't be all things to all people. So first the libraries tried something pretty heavy-handed. They denied access to richer people outright! That's right. Whenever the scanner showed that your income exceeded a certain amount, entrance was denied. I guess they figured that the wealthy could get along without free, tax-supported services. Poor people, on the other hand, the ones who *couldn't* afford to pay for their own library and information services, could get in free and use as much as they want. Hey, you're lucky. Two years ago, you couldn't even have gotten in here, no matter how much you had in your account."

"And did the poor come in and use the free library?"

"A few of them did. I don't know. I didn't see many that looked like poverty types. Most of our patrons always were and still are people pretty much like you. You know, well-to-do. For a while, the poor were issued information stamps, administered by one of those awful government bureaucracies. But that idea didn't work any better than the other bright schemes they tried."

"And who establishes the so-called poverty line?"

"The government does, and every month it changes the figures. Services are still free for those whose ID cards indicate that they fall below the line established by the United States Department of Welfare. And because no fixed credit amount defining poverty is built into the program, it's always current, based on the previous month's percentages of the population. Family income information is derived from the previous year's federal tax records and is encoded on the citizen's ID card. When people want admission to the library, the automatic scanners at the entrance determine the citizen's fee status and either grant free admission or deduct the appropriate amount from the citizen's credit account."

"Didn't anybody fight this measure?"

Artie looks at him in disbelief. "You really got yourself buried out there on the red planet, didn't ya? Well, since you're asking, yes, there was what seemed like months of debate and dispute about this legislation back when it came before Congress. Originally, the fee status was keyed to specific dollar amounts. Then, when the dollar disappeared and electronic credits became the law of the land, it was easier to do it electronically and to let the values float. Big deal! Didn't change a thing, I'm telling you. Representatives of depressed economic areas, minority groups, mostly, argued that a fee structure sent the wrong message or some such garbage. Most of 'em in Washington thought that the poverty level shouldn't be geared to some arbitrary number of credits each year, but instead ought to be based on percentages of the population. Hey, don't ask me about the mathematics of the thing! The five happiest years of my life are the ones I spent trying to get out of seventh grade."

"Where was I? Oh, yeah, information stamps. Then things really went to hell! The federal government decided to get into the act in its usual clumsy, bureaucratic fashion. They had this scheme that looked pretty good on paper but that didn't work out at all in reality: information stamps. I can't believe that you didn't hear about this up on Mars!"

"Oh, I heard about it, but we didn't have anything like that up there, so it didn't mean anything to me. Go on. Tell me how it worked."

"Ahh, let me think." He falls silent for a few moments, his thumb scratching the light stubble on his chin. "I think information stamps were based on the same principle that food stamps operated under since they first hit the scene, whenever that was. 1970 or something, I dunno. Through this method, the library charged a per-visit fee for admission or use, but families with income below the poverty level were sent quarterly packets of information stamps, which could be used for admission to the library building, sorta like traded for research or reference questions, or for borrowing library materials." He rummages around behind the counter and comes up with another sign somewhat the worse for wear, which, he says, used to hang in the place now occupied by the one bearing the library's fee structure. The sign contains the following table:

RIVERTOWN PUBLIC LIBRARY:
INFORMATION STAMP EXCHANGE RATES

Family Income per capita*	Quarterly stamps per capita*
over 75,000 credits annually	none
between 50,000 and 75,000	4
between 25,000 and 50,000	8
below poverty level (25,000)	16

* minimum age = 8 years

"But the thing of it is," Artie continues, "information stamps never caught on the way food stamps did. I'll tell you how useless they were: nobody even wanted to steal 'em. So, despite a big advertising campaign, libraries had plenty of trouble getting people to use 'em at all. I know ours did! Seems like the government couldn't demonstrate to people that information, itself, was an important, valuable commodity and could help folks conduct their daily lives better. What's more, all that bureaucracy cost the government all out of proportion to the benefits received and after endless Congressional debate the plan was scrapped. I forget just when. Nobody ever talks about it anymore on the newsvids. Embarrassed, I guess."

"So that's how we came up with this plan, that turns the cost-structure around, shifting the burden of getting information from the poor to the wealthy as a form of rationing. Persons below the poverty line, under this arrangement, get free access to all library services simply by passing their IDs under this scanner. Rich people's cards look exactly like the ones that poor folks get, only their cards are tied into their bank balances and savings accounts, with the fees for library use subtracted from their accounts automatically. Some system, huh? Robbin' somebody blind at one time or another." He snorts derisively and looks around as if for a good place to spit.

"But wait! It gets worse. The government's bright boys next came up with a plan that's as close to offering bribes as you ever seen. To get people to use their library cards, a deal was set up so that users were automatically entitled to corresponding units of rationed food substances. So let's say a kid wants some ice cream. Now, you gotta remember that real ice cream is in short supply since all those radioactive cattle had to be destroyed back in '97, right? And children don't seem to like the various synthetics. Hell, who does? So kids started getting ice cream in exchange for library use. Then we figured out that kids were only comin' to the library so they could get the ice cream coupons. Or most of 'em anyway. I mean, library use ought to be its own reward, shouldn't it? I may not be a college graduate, but I know that much. Well, that was another idea down the tubes." Artie chuckles reflectively. Then he continues.

A mobile mall of the future. The retail stores radiating out from the central core fold up into large trailers. The stores can travel from mall to mall, hook up to the central core, and start selling.

Just the spot for tomorrow's single-purpose branch library. Illustration: Selame Design, Newton, Massachusetts. From the February 1981 issue of *The Futurist*. Used with permission.

SOME THINGS TO ALL

"Other towns are doin' other things. Like Center City, which is maybe ninety, a hundred klicks west of here. In their library, they let you in for free and you can use whatever you find there for absolutely nothing. But it's kind of like one of those old good news, bad news jokes. Remember them? The good news is all that free service. The bad news is that the range of services is extremely limited. See, Center City has the big music conservatory. Well, their public library's whole collection is music. Sheet music, records, videos, instruments, even holograms. They got everything, but only in the one area. That means if you live in Center City and you want to get hold of some stock or consumer information, they don't have it and you can't get it there. You want fiction? You want to borrow a feature film? Or take the kids to a story hour, or get something in the area of science and technology? Forget about it. They don't have it. They're polite, of course. But they're firm. If you ask where the novels are, they give you this sheet of bookstore names and book rental agencies. You want a movie? Every video store or club in the area is on a sheet. Anything for the kids? They have a list of every agency or child care store in the area. But if you've come for something musical, you've come to the right place. That's what they do and they do it well, but that's *all* they do and there's no use asking for more or different stuff. They've become a real specialty operation."

"The way I figure it, that library, just like this one here, decided that they couldn't go into the new century trying to be all things to all people like they were before. Not only couldn't they afford it, but they didn't really see a market for it. But unlike our library, which decided to charge for library services, the Center City library came up with some sort of stirring patriotic claptrap about how libraries ought to be free, how you shouldn't need money in your pocket or purse to get in, and how that was the way it ought to be, now and forevermore. Sorta brings a tear to your eye, don't it?" Mockingly, he pretends to dry his eyes.

Russ takes the opportunity to get a question in edgewise. "So they don't charge for anything they do, but they don't do all that much, right?"

"You got it. And I read about some other libraries in other cities that have done some variations on that theme. The one in Millersville just focuses on children. Once you're sixteen or so the library isn't for you, so don't even ask. And Connersburg's library closed all of its walk-in operations, but they run a pretty good reference service by telephone. Just another approach to a problem, I guess." He sits staring into the middle distance, looking at nothing, until Russ brings him back with a question.

"So I guess I have my choice, right? I can pay the price for full service here or go to another town and pay nothing."

"Yeah, nothing, but only if you want specific services. At least we still offer a full-service library. Another thing you can do is to get poorer. Once the central computer has you down as eligible for poverty-line services, you can get in here and use anything you see absolutely free."

"Let me understand this," Russ persists. "Suppose I want reference service, but I don't want to pay any eighty credits a day and I don't want to go over to Center City. What do I do?"

"That's an easy one. Try one of the private information providers. We have them all listed here on this viewer, together with the things they do and the rates they charge. Or pay 9,000 credits for the whole year. That's less than twenty-five credits a day, if you don't count that we're closed on Sundays."

"Funny, I guess it pays to be poor."

"I don't know about that. Try living on the crummy salary I get for sitting here at the door and explaining it all to people like you. Then you'll believe what that lady used to say. Something like 'I've been rich and I've been poor, and rich is better.'"

"I believe it already," Russ answers. "And there's no way I can get in today without having all those credits subtracted from my account?"

"Not unless you wanna take your chances and leap over the turnstile. I wouldn't try to stop you, but I wouldn't advise it, personally. Our security robot is very fast and pretty good at catching gate crashers. Three or four a week think they're gonna sneak past me or whoever is working this desk. Before you can even say, 'stop that guy!' old Security has 'em in restraints and is calling the cops to take 'em away and book 'em for trespass. And that carries a much bigger fine than your daily admission to this building. Also, repeat offenders draw mandatory jail terms. No, you want in? You pay. Or you come back when you're poor. Otherwise, here's the list of private companies and Center City is thataway." He jerks his thumb over his shoulder, still grinning pleasantly.

"Yeah. I see how it is. Well, it's good to be home again, I guess, even if things change and not always for the better." Dejectedly, Russ walks out of the building, wondering if the fuel units recorded on the ration card sector of his ID are sufficient to take him to Center City and bring him back today. He walks down the sidewalk, kicking at small stones and trying to remember all the words to that very old song that ended with the words "there's no place like home."

> The information you have is not what you want.
> The information you want is not what you need.
> The information you need is not available.
> —Finagle's Law

Circles show electromagnetic pulse ground coverage for nuclear bursts at 100, 300, and 500 kilometers above the United States. Within these circles, strength of the pulse would be at least 25,000 volts per meter, with peak fields of 50,000 volts. Courtesy *Bulletin of the Atomic Scientists*, March 1983. Used with permission.

10
EMP

A Post-Holocaust Scenario

Tumbling slowly through the blackness of space, the satellite moves to a point exactly 330 miles above Omaha, Nebraska. Suddenly it vaporizes in a silent nuclear fireball. In less than a second, the entire United States is bathed with a high voltage wave called EMP (for electromagnetic pulse). The country's power grid fails, most communications from coast to coast are knocked out, almost every computer system in the U.S. is damaged or destroyed.

          —John L. Kirkley, 1981

July 12, 2018

Shortly after midnight, Washington, D.C. time, the lone Soviet missile arches gracefully over the north pole and speeds southward over the Canadian wilderness and across the United States's northern border. By the time the startled American president can be awakened from slumber and apprised of the situation, civilian and military advisers are shouting contradictory advice and the government's automated Expert Defense System has only time enough to lay out several options for retaliation. But the president has precious little time and squanders it pondering options, seemingly paralyzed with indecision and shock. At precisely 12:23 a.m., Eastern Standard Time, on July 12, 2018, the multipartite warhead bursts over southeastern Nebraska, creating, as it was intended to do, an electromagnetic pulse (EMP) which spreads over virtually all of the continental United States, changing forever the course of history.

Perhaps the world should be congratulated on the fact that the weapons used did not kill, accounting for a considerably more humane outcome than what might have happened had not cooler heads prevailed. In any event, when World War III ends just about six hours after it began, casualties on both sides are judged extremely light in terms of human life lost or incapacitated. However, the machines which increasingly have sustained human life and supported or carried out human endeavor are out of action for hundreds of years by all estimates. In minutes, human society has been driven back to its condition prior to the start of the eighteenth century.

The irony is that no machines have been destroyed. There is not a mark on them. People are also little affected physically. But every square centimeter of the nation is bombarded with enough charged neutrons to bring all electro-mechanical activity to a screeching halt.

Such people who do die lose their lives in automobiles which stall, their onboard computers inoperative, or in airplanes which are airborne at the time of the detonation and fall heavily to earth, their guidance computers suddenly blank. Panic and chaos in the streets and buildings of America kill perhaps five thousand more, but the aftermath of the single explosion is an almost eerie silence and little more.

> When electromagnetic pulse—the brief burst of intense electromagnetic energy generated by nuclear explosions high above the earth—was first detected during early atmospheric tests, scientists considered it only a potential nuisance. But in 1962 ... a detonation over Johnston Atoll knocked out street lights and triggered burglar alarms 800 miles away in Honolulu. EMP's devastating impact on electronics systems has since become a major military concern.... Several large high-altitude nuclear

explosions might render unprotected equipment and systems inoperative over an area as large as the continental United States.

—David M. Kennedy, 1985

Residents of the mid-sized city of Rivertown in the midwestern United States have so many things to worry about they can't quite assimilate and accept what has happened to them. Although deaths and injuries are few, the effects of the bomb are far-reaching. Air-conditioning is inoperative, as are refrigeration and all but the oldest automobiles (only those not fitted with computers). Since EMP has interfered with the transmission of electricity, all power sources are dead and may well remain so for a time exceeding the lifetimes of all city residents. Streetlights are dead. Telephones are no more than strangely shaped paperweights. Traffic signals swing over the street on the warm winds beneath the peculiarly orange-colored sky. Hospitals are without power. Stores quickly sell out of kerosene lamps and batteries for portable power. Local radio and television stations can't broadcast instructions to civilians for dealing with the emergency, and even if they could, only those with battery-operated receivers would be able to tune in.

Lillian Harris, director of the city's library, has had a rough day. She spent most of it running around on foot trying to ascertain that her children and husband are alive and unharmed. Reassured at least this much, she has fed her family from the contents of the kitchen freezer (in this hot weather, without electricity things are likely to spoil quickly). Now she gets to wondering what's happening down at the library. The public library is the last thing on most people's minds on this unique July day, but it is always on Lillian's mind whatever is going on in the real world.

Her twelve-year-old daughter Beth, no longer terrified and now frankly curious about the day's events, asks her some very pointed questions, which she does her best to field.

"Mom, what happened this morning? Why is the electricity shut off and why did the sky turn that funny color?"

"I can only tell you what the government has managed to make known to us. A big bomb went off about six hundred miles from here, 'way up in the sky. Just one bomb, but that's all it takes, nowadays. That would explain the sky's color, I suppose, and as for electricity, I think we can forget all about that for the rest of our lives. From what I've heard, the bomb totaled that forever."

"Who did it?"

"The Soviets, I guess."

"But why?"

"I don't know. I've never understood war. The two biggest kids on the block—eventually, they have to fight."

"Did we get 'em back?"

"Yes, I guess you could say we did. After the bomb went off, our government exploded one just like it over central Russia. That evened the score. Then, and this is almost too good to be true, our two leaders somehow got in touch with each other and decided to call the whole thing off before people began getting killed by the millions. That's the only sensible thing they did today."

"So, the Russians' electronics don't work, either?"

"Hard to tell."

"What kind of bomb was it? I thought bombs blew things up and knocked down buildings for miles around and set everything on fire."

"Some bombs do. This was a different kind of bomb. This one wasn't supposed to hurt people or damage buildings. It just destroys computer programs and messes around with electricity. I suppose we ought to be grateful."

"Did this bomb kill people?"

"Not really, if you don't count the ones who were up in airplanes or out on the highway when it went off. Some of them got killed when their engines failed, or so I heard."

"Do you still have a job? Is there still a library on Monroe Street?"

"Interesting question. I guess I'd better take a ride over there later on and find out."

Late in the afternoon, Lillian borrows her daughter's bicycle and pedals four miles to the library, reasonably sure it's still there, but curious and fearful of what she may find in it. She hops on the bicycle, armed with a four-cell flashlight and a long-handled umbrella to ward off animals. She has noticed that animals have behaved strangely all day. Dogs howl incessantly, cats have disappeared, and the fish in her aquarium have spent the day speeding around their bowl, looking frightened. She can readily appreciate why anyone is frightened today. The high wind caused by the explosion has downed some telephone poles and power lines, but it doesn't take her long to figure out that there is no danger from them, nor is there likely to be for the next thousand years or so. An eerie orange phosphorescence surrounds everything, yet the air is warm and breathable and there is no real evidence that a nuclear device has exploded in the substratosphere early this morning. Actually, considering the circumstances, it has become a rather nice day.

Astride the bicycle, she picks her way around crashed cars and stalled traffic, finally arriving at the library perhaps half an hour before twilight. She sees, upon letting herself in with her key, that the gloomy interior of the building is not any different from the way it was at closing time yesterday. It is, however, very quiet. No swish of air-conditioning or the ventilator fans can be heard. Her footsteps echo loudly in absolute silence as she walks into her own office. By reflex, she clicks the light switch up and down a few times before she remembers why it doesn't work. It is hot and close in the building and Lillian would like to open a window, but the old library was built around 1970, and like many other public buildings of the time is hermetically sealed to prevent dust and moisture from entering.

Just out of curiosity, she picks up her desk telephone. Dead. She remembers the time in '08 or '09 that a tornado hit the city's main power station and the library was without power for thirty-eight hours. For her, it had been a major headache; for the staff, a paid holiday. But at least the telephones had worked. Now, there were no signs of life, no sounds, nothing. Lillian hears voices outside. Strange. In her fifteen years of working in the building, it has never been so silent that such quiet outside sounds could be heard.

She moves through the technical services area, shining her flashlight's beam around her as she walks. Rows of machines stand silent, just where they stopped when the power was abruptly and permanently cut off. Lillian thinks of the hundreds of credits worth of frozen food in her home refrigerator, wondering whether her family can eat it all before it spoils. Ice (or perhaps gasoline) will soon be the currency and value unit around here, at least until winter comes and ice can be made the old-fashioned way, by letting river water stand in block molds overnight. Winter won't be so bad, she hopes, with the countryside full of trees which can be burned in fireplaces and converted stoves. At least the bomb couldn't take that away.

Lillian knows that the few pre-1990 cars without computerized microprocessors will probably still run, needing only gas to operate. Her family's cars, however, date from 2009 and run, unfortunately, on solid-state microprocessors in their engines. They will have to rely on bicycles and walking. She sighs. It might have been worse. There are no burned or destroyed buildings, no people vaporized from the flash and blast of a nuclear explosion. No hospitals full of corpses and burned, mangled bodies. It certainly could have been worse.

Yet Lillian has a library to run, and hasn't the slightest idea of how she's going to do it. She knows that libraries existed long, long before the advent of electrical power. With a little ingenuity and hard work, they will continue to exist, or at least *hers* will.

Taking inventory, she finds that the bookshelves and books are exactly as they were before the bomb blast. Perhaps a series of rooftop skylights will solve the lighting problem during the daytime. And for nighttime? If battery-powered lighting is not feasible, perhaps torches made of sticks wrapped in oil-soaked rags, just like the ones used in Roman libraries two thousand years ago, can be placed along the walls, far, of course, from the books and other materials. The library's outstanding collection of films is unusable, as are recordings of all types except those which can be operated in the library's battery-powered players. If portable power packs can be set up for the library's electrical equipment, it would almost be business as usual.

One particularly vexing problem is that of the catalog, which serves as an index and finding guide to the collection, together with the various files and indexes which are available on disk. Lillian remembers the day when the decision was made to switch over to automated catalog terminals. She also remembers, with a rueful shudder, how on her recommendation the library board voted not only to replace but to dispose of the old card catalog entirely rather than permitting it to remain, albeit in the basement. Who could have foreseen what would happen?

Now, she knows, her array of computer catalog terminals is no more useful than the cinderblocks in the walls, even if the information stored on the disks had not been wiped clean. Still, she decides she will wait a while before deciding whether to throw the machines out or to try to rig something with powerpack batteries. And of course a card catalog will have to be recreated because without one the library will be nothing more than a haphazard collection of books, arranged only loosely according to the preexisting classification scheme devised over 125 years ago by a man named Dewey. She knows there will be no shortage of labor now that everyone who operated the machines is out of work, but she dreads it all the same. And where to find the required number of manual typewriters in good working order is a problem she can't even begin to think about without getting a headache.

Might as well write off the circulation system, she reflects sadly. Not to mention the air-conditioning, the computers, and the robots that the library had relied upon, never seriously worrying that they might have to do without them. Elevators aren't going to work any more, but she figures that isn't all bad. She can use the exercise of climbing the stairs several times a day, but something will have to be done for elderly and disabled citizens. A series of ramps might be built by carpenters, she supposes, or some kind of pulley lift and window apparatus.

She walks over to SAM, the library's utility robot, who until yesterday evening was constantly busy retrieving books and periodical issues, answering questions, dispensing advice, directing patrons, and handling various forms of transactions. SAM droops listlessly, his power cord still plugged into a wall recharger which will probably never be of any use to him again. His programmers have outfitted him with enough random-access memory and ergonomic interfaces to provide him with an extremely congenial, attractive, helpful, and sympathetic personality, especially when compared with some of the human co-workers Lillian had to deal with, and she is going to miss him sorely, now that he's quite literally dead.

SAM could do so many things. He could translate between English and over forty foreign languages and diagnose and treat medical illnesses. He knew the words and music to over 140,000 songs, arias, airs, and themes; could remember and tell flawlessly over 300,000 jokes and stories; and even provide a very efficient one-unit security force when necessary. She remembers the time that a huge, musclebound man, drunk and angry over something or other he never tried to explain, pulled out a club of some kind and attempted to bash everyone in the library over the head with it. SAM had glided over on silent casters and disarmed him from behind without effort. Then, without injury to the enraged man, SAM immobilized him gently while summoning a police cruiser to take him away. Afterwards, the ever-modest SAM credited others with the detainment of the man.

Still, she tells herself, although much may be gone, much remains. Lillian, never a quitter, resolves to run as efficient a library as she can given the severe constraints. Somewhere in all the information and knowledge stored in this building, she believes there is the answer to the problem of getting an alternative power source. Until then, she resolves she is going to provide the shocked and frightened post-EMP citizens of the city with the best library the seventeenth century has ever seen until such time as the twenty-first century library is ready once again to emerge triumphant. This time, she thinks, maybe the world can figure out how to avoid the consequences of militarism and nationalism and remember what's really important in life.

Lost in thought, she gives the defunct robot a last sad tweak on the faceplate, muttering "So long, SAM," and walks on, shining the flashlight ahead of her down the long aisles of bookstacks. This library will still have a place in the life of the community, she promises, maybe even an enhanced role in the rebuilding of technology. In the meantime, she'll do the best job possible of restoring what she can and improvising the rest. Lord knows, people need knowledge now more than ever. As for the hardware and software that ran the library this morning, she'll worry about that tomorrow.

Wandering out into the evening, Lillian reflects on the tragic waste of war and the folly of humanity. The eerie glow that seems to come from the sky has changed to a soft lavender color with the darkness, and makes it as easy to see as if it were a snow-covered night. At least she won't need a light on her long journey, she thinks, trying to look at the bright side. Nor will anyone else for the next ten thousand years.

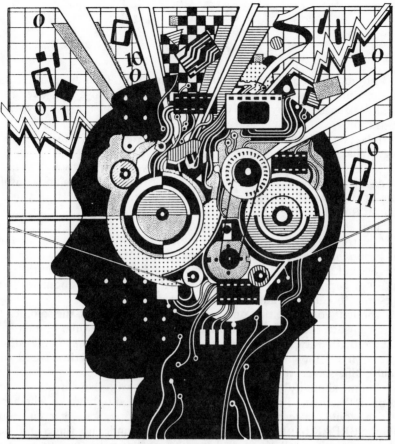

Future equipment will make it possible to record and capture brain waves and thoughts on cassettes and play them back. Illustration courtesy Clipper Creative Art Service®, copyright Dynamic Graphics, Inc., Peoria, Illinois.

11
The Experience Parlour

Be careful what you wish for; you might get it.
— Variously attributed

March 4, 2009

Just about dinnertime, a small, smiling man bounds into the large building which used to be the Rivertown Public Library, and over to the central desk in the lobby, over which hangs a sign which reads "Experience Registration."

He says to the woman behind the desk, "Hey there, Marge! How's it going? What's new? What've you got for me today?"

"Hello, Larry," she responds. "I thought you'd be in today. Tuesday's your day, isn't it? Well, lemme see, here." She thumbs a button and consults a listing of titles which appears on the screen of her console. "Have you done 'Amazon Rain Forest' yet?"

"Two weeks ago. That was a good one! When that 25-foot snake dropped out of the tree onto the guy in front of me and started squeezing the life out of him, I thought I was about to have a heart attack! And then when we got to that riverbank! Whew! I had thought that piranha were only about the size of goldfish or guppies. Guess I didn't know that they got to be about yea long!" he gestures, holding his hands about a foot apart.

"Thought you'd like that one," chuckles Marge. "Scared me so much that I almost pushed the BREAK button, but, y'know, after a while I kinda forget about the BREAK capability. Like it isn't there! Like I'm *really* in the Amazon jungle with all the heat and humidity and dangerous critters and bugs. Yecchh!" She shivers at the memory.

"Tell me about it," agrees Larry. "When I was with that surrounded scout platoon in 'Vietnam, Tet Offensive,' I was concerned only about whether the Vietcong would waste me or I'd step on a mine first. I never even thought about the BREAK button. Even though it was just under my fingertip, I never thought to use it at all. I mean, I wasn't just witnessing war up close and personal, I was *there*! Know what I mean?"

Marge, nodding her head, returns to her computerized file. "Here's one of the new ones. Haven't tried it out myself, but Sandy in the history and travel division did when it first came in and said that it was so realistic that it took her ten minutes of just lying there before she could get her mind to return to the here and now after the experience ended, and another twenty minutes to stop shivering. It's called 'Climbing Mount Everest,' and she advised me to dress warmly when I go into the booth. Says that even though she knows that it's always climate controlled and comfortable in the booth, she like to froze to death on the way up and down that mountain. To say nothing of that *thing* out there! But I don't wanna spoil it for you, so I'd better say no more."

"Thing? What thing out there?" asks Larry.

"Like I say, I don't wanna spoil it for you." Marge weighs the experience cassette in her hands. It looks like a videocassette, the kind that has been around for over twenty years.

"I've been using these things once a week for six months and I still don't know how they work," says Larry. "Tell me, in words I can understand, how they make these things."

"I told you last week! Remember?" Marge waves her arms impatiently. "About fifteen years ago, somebody in one of the sciences figured out that experiences can be captured on tape just like sights and sounds! So as long as whomever is recording these experiences is willing to wear a large and cumbersome helmet which wires his or her brain up to a recorder, the experience can be captured on tape and replayed into somebody else's brain. So whatever the guy who's wearing the recorder experiences or sees or hears or smells or tastes when the tape is on record will now be part of your consciousness when the tape is placed in a player and the electrodes are taped to your skull when you hit the PLAY button. For things that have already happened, there's some kinda process called a time-warp simulation. Don't ask! It'd take a genius to explain it. I just work here, y'know? Larry, if I understood how it worked, I wouldn't be a wage-slave here at the library. Oops! I mean here at the parlour. But it works, it really works! Let it go at that."

"Absolutely incredible is what it is!" breathes Larry. "More realistic than anything. Well, I'd like to stand here and chat, Marge, but I gotta get home tonight to watch the kids while Gretchen comes over here for her appointment, so let me get on with it. I'll take 'Mount Everest.'"

"Oh, I think you're going to like this one a lot. Take booth number 142, and remember, don't take off your jacket. You'll thank me for that. Just signal me on the intercom when you're comfortable and ready to roll and I'll boot it up for you. That's ten credits. Cash or charge?"

After giving Marge the standard fee and signing the standard medical release form, Larry walks down corridors lined on both sides by numbered doors until he finds number 142. He enters, closes the door, begins to slip off his suit jacket, and stops, smiling, remembering Marge's warning, and leaves it on. Removing his glasses, he places them on a convenient shelf and loosens his tie. Finally, he eases himself down onto the comfortably padded recliner and draws the helmet/headset gently down over his brows. He is ready. Dimming the lights with the rheostat close to his left hand, he toggles the intercom switch. "Okay, Marge. Let'er rip!" Larry exclaims, happily anticipating the pleasure of being in on a historic and dangerous event, a famous first, without ever leaving his warm, padded recliner in a booth at the Rivertown Experience Parlour.

"Happy trails," Marge's voice comes from the ceiling speaker as she inserts the "Everest" cassette into a slot and pushes the PLAY button marked 142 on the master console behind the desk. She adds something else, but Larry cannot hear in the roar of the wind coming up the side of the vast ice crevasse he's staring down into. Hillary is shouting at him, his goggled eyes unreadable, but his voice indicates some irritation. "Wind's rising, old man. Going to be bloody cold tonight, wouldn't you say? Best camp here while we've the daylight."

"Huh?" says Larry, confused. Sir Edmund Hillary is entirely right. It is cold already, a penetrating cold driven by the wind through the heavy, layered clothing he wears. "Snap out of it, Lawrence!" says Hillary, angrily. "You're well aware that the success of this expedition, and the welfare of each man in it depends on constant attention to detail and the utmost concentration! If you go wool gathering, old Tenzing and I might as well leave you here at 23,000 feet, for you'll be no bloody use to us any higher!"

"Sorry, Sir Edmund," says Larry, now fully aware of the critical nature of his full participation in this great adventure. The brutal wind seems to be whipping the words out of his mouth, so he says them again, much louder. When Hillary acknowledges his words with a curt "Right!" Larry takes a moment to look around him, wonderingly. He is standing with two other men on a small flat shelf in what seems to be an otherwise steeply angled ice fissure. From up here, the entire Himalayan range stretches to the horizon, the snow-covered mountains becoming blue and indistinct as they recede into the distance. In front of him is the legendary Sir Edmund Hillary, the intrepid explorer whose three-man expedition is seeking to stand atop Mount Everest, where no man has ever stood before. The third man is a small, dark, and silent man named Tenzing Norkay, a Sherpa guide from Nepal. His skilled hands, despite three thicknesses of gloves and mittens, are busily setting up a three-man orange canvas tent in the meager shelter of a glacial outcropping of rock.

Larry is aware that they are at 23,000 feet and tomorrow they're going to be much higher. He looks up thoughtfully at the snow-covered summit, pink in the last rays of a feeble sun. The day after tomorrow they'll stand on the highest spot in the world, if they don't die tonight in the relentless freezing wind and occasional avalanches. And, he reminds himself, if there is no Abominable Snowman waiting in an ice cave somewhere to throw them down a crevasse or devour them like men eat chickens. Larry shivers at that thought and tries to dismiss it from his head. He has duties of his own before Tenzing, Sir Edmund, and he can crawl into that tent, button its doorflap, and attempt to sleep huddled together for warmth. He must cook some hot food from their dwindling supplies and make plenty of strong, boiling-hot coffee. Shivering uncontrollably, he hunches down within his parka, trying to light the stove. If only the wind would quit for one minute, he thinks wearily, just one windless minute. How can it blow perpetually? For the forty-fifth or maybe the ninety-third time today he wonders how he let himself get talked into this assignment. He remembers the big press conference just before the three of them set off from Katmandu, warm and green in the morning light. He remembers Hillary's clever rejoinder when some reporter asked him why he was out to climb Mount Everest. "Because it's there, old man!" he had said to general laughter. Now it's here, and Larry's at 23,000 feet, with the sun going down rapidly in the west and the temperature falling fast from just under freezing to an anticipated 35 degrees below, Fahrenheit.

Despite his overall physical fitness and his preclimb conditioning, his breathing is labored as he fixes them a meager repast. It takes a while for him to remember that at this height everything is more work because the air is oxygen-poor. And it's only going to get worse as they climb to the summit, he reminds himself.

An hour later, after a brief high-protein meal and three cups of coffee, and needing sleep for the arduous days ahead, he zips himself into his down-filled sleeping bag, wearing all of his clothes except for his boots. Later, somewhere between waking and sleep, he hears an unusual noise against the backdrop of the perpetually howling wind. He lifts his head and looks at his unmoving, sleeping companions. Fully awake, he lies there trying to ignore the noises he hears over the wind's shriek and roar, but the sort of growling, animal sound grows louder. Larry knows no animals live at 23,000 feet, but his ears tell him that something or someone is snarling just outside the tent. Reluctantly, noting that his companions are still asleep, he crawls to the button-down door of the tent and opens it. Unbelievable cold surgically cuts his face, freezing the tears in his eyes. Donning his protective goggles, he sees little in the darkness but he hears the sounds, louder now, as if something is disturbing the remains of their campfire. As his vision adjusts to the snow-covered mountainside in the middle of night, he could swear he sees something huge, white, and shaggy, but indistinct moving slowly towards the tent. Then a pair of eyes reflect the moonlight, like those of a dog caught in a car's headlights, frightening him beyond description. There *is* something out there and whatever it is, it's coming this way! Clumsily, he heaves his exhausted body out of his sleeping bag. "Sir Edmund! Tenzing!" he shrieks. "Wake up and bring the rifles! We have company!..."

Twenty minutes later, a trembling Larry lies alone in booth 142 sipping a thoughtfully provided cup of hot tea with extra sugar. The climate-control readout on his console tells him that the booth temperature stands at 68 degrees Fahrenheit, yet he shivers uncontrollably. The intercom's squawk startles him as Marge's voice is piped into the room. "So, Larry," she asks jocularly. "How did it go? Did you get down off the mountain all right?"

"Guess so," he mumbles. "But jeez, I thought it was real, Marge! I mean I wasn't just watching a film about it, I was *there*! The cold went into my bones. Hillary spoke to me. I saw the world from a place where only the most daring ever go. And I think, I'd swear! I think ... that I might have seen ..." He pauses. "Well, I don't know just what I saw. Something was out there, but by the time I woke up the others, it was gone. If it had ever been there, that is."

"Can you get up, now?" says Marge's solicitous voice through the speaker. "Sorry, but we need the booth. But next week, for a change of pace, how'd you like to play the middle linebacker position on the 1998 Chicago Bears in the Super Bowl against New England? I remember you weren't much of a jock back in high school. Here's your chance to cover yourself with glory, sack that quarterback, get carried off the field by your fans, and you won't even have to change out of your street clothes. Shall I book it for you? Same time, Larry?"

"Um, yeah. Thanks, Marge. Sounds good to me," Larry murmurs distractedly, rising at last, his mind on other things. Those glowing eyes and that penetrating cold! So real! Shrugging his shoulders, he straightens his tie, slips on and ties his shoes, and goes out past the rows of booths containing his fellow citizens. He ventures out into the cool March evening, toward dinner with his wife and kids in his rented apartment on the city's west side. It's been a tiring day, he decides, and I think I'm going to turn in early.

EVOLUTION OF THE
EXPERIENCE PARLOUR

It's the same building but everything in it is different. The sign over the door, which used to say "Public Library," now reads "Experience Parlour." The staff now call themselves *experience facilitators* or *neotravel agents.* The library's official listing in the directory of city agencies now is "Municipal Experience Parlour."

Books and audiovisual media were the stock and trade of the public library during the twentieth century, but in this century people's lives demand more involvement than could be afforded by two-dimensional film or pages. They seek "all-at-onceness" and actual participation in the experiences they witness. People come to the experience parlour for a variety of reasons, some to seek escape and others to pump excitement into humdrum lives. The institution has gradually become a place where they can get release from tedium or apathy without jeopardizing their jobs, their personal safety, or their marriages. People don't just want entertainment anymore, they want roles.

A survey was taken of users after the first year of operation. Users defined their principal reasons for coming as: (1) to escape routine, (2) to test a new lifestyle before abandoning their own, (3) to be entertained in novel, involving ways, (4) to be challenged by different or exacting circumstances, (5) to learn (or learn about) something new, and (6) to realize fantasies which, for a multiplicity of reasons, will have to remain fantasies.

The programmed experience grew out of some popular television shows of the last century. In the early days of network television, a weekly show called "The Millionaire" gave an ordinary man or woman a cashier's check for one million dollars, to do with as he or she wished, provided certain conditions were agreed to and met. Many people, however, wound up wishing they had never answered the knock on the door from the man with the million. In the 1980s, the largely forgettable "Fantasy Island" was based on the interesting premise of buying a fantasy as a type of vacation. These people were flown to a remote tropical paradise where, amid scenic splendor, waterfalls, coconut palms, and attractive companions, their ultimate fantasies and dreams could be realized. Frequently, these fantasies met with unpredictable or unsatisfactory results.

"Lifestyles of the Rich and Famous" was another 1980s show which made it possible to see or imagine more clearly how the very wealthy lived, played, and entertained themselves. This program often aroused feelings of unrest in consumers.

Other attempts to create fantasies and occasionally make them happen included state and national lotteries, where millions of dollars could be won for a comparatively modest investment.

These entertainments, however, fell short of affording involvement. The pleasure or pain of living out one's fantasies was purely vicarious, as one watched others coping with sudden fortune or fantasy fulfillment. By the turn of the twenty-first century, people expressed a wish that they not just watch people undergoing wish realization, but that they actually *become* these people, under conditions as realistic as possible.

Therefore, the public library, on the road to making itself over, changed to accommodate people's changing desires and needs. Although the reasons for such a change were many and varied, the main reason was that the public library, wishing to survive in times of economic uncertainty, felt compelled to undergo wholesale metamorphosis in order to achieve that survival.

People want roles and the experience parlour, inheritor of the library's legacy, gives those roles to them thanks to some startling developments in information and entertainment technology. Today the library no longer resembles the original building. Its rectilinear rows of bookshelves and reading areas have given way to corridors lined with experience booths. Each booth is equipped with a comfortable reclining lounge chair which bears a strong resemblance to the type of chair used in dentistry before the advent of chemical drilling, a helmet/headset with several attachments to fit all, some medical devices to monitor heart rate and other vital signs, players for appropriate music, a color organ for creating tone and hue, and a console providing, among other things, a BREAK button which immediately ends the experience. Additionally, there are shelves, a table for personal belongings, and a changing area, toilet-equipped, for getting comfortable. Each session in the booth lasts thirty minutes although temporal sense is sometimes suspended or altered when the client is under the influence of the experience. Privacy is assured, and attendants have been trained only to monitor vital signs and to see to the correct functioning of the equipment. They will not normally interfere with the experience. As a form of rationing, and to cover expenses, each client may visit the experience parlour no more than once a week and must pay ten dollars for the experience. Most say it is money well spent, leaving the client (patron, like library, is a word which no longer applies, and is seldom heard) refreshed.

Social critics, however, are warning of a growing phenomenon of experience addiction. The contrast between the grim reality of day-to-day life in the first decade of the twenty-first century and the exciting, often indulgent fantasies experienced by those in the booths is creating a form of addiction. Some clients, rather than emerging refreshed from their experiences, find themselves deeply disappointed and distraught, as when awakened from a good dream to a life of worry and reality. There are reports of people attempting to exceed their allotment of visits or breaking into the library at night to use the equipment, and the library staff worries about both the social/ethical and security implications of this phenomenon.

There is much to consider in permitting this service to exist. The first concern is for the personal safety and well-being of the client or user. One of several variables is the condition of the equipment. Faulty wiring or defective programming could lead to a traumatic accident. One woman in Maryland recently sued her local library for malpractice and personal injury, claiming that the experience headset she was given was defective, showing her the same scene at five-second intervals for the full thirty minutes rather than proceeding sequentially from potential danger to gratifying conclusions. She charged the city of Baltimore with faulty inspection and the experience parlour with criminal negligence. Claiming that she suffered extensive post-experience trauma including nightmares, insomnia, inability to relax, and certain unspecified marital problems, she has sued for $2 million. The city counters that it is free of blame because it did exercise reasonable care in inspecting both equipment and programmed experiences, that accidents can and do happen, and that the woman signed the standard release form of her own free will. The resultant bad publicity has caused all municipal experience parlours to rethink their safety precautions, and a bill before Congress requires that no one may use an experience cassette before it has been tested by at least two parlour staff members.

The battle rages over such interactive media, and everyone seems to have an opinion. Still, the allure of the parlour continues to pack people in, and the Rivertown Experience Parlour has a booked-up schedule for weeks to come. Last week, the facility's director submitted a proposal to the city for expansion of room and facilities to accommodate the demand.

A number of nagging legal questions remain concerning experience parlours and their packaged experiences. These are but a few: (1) Who is at fault and responsible if the machine is defective? (2) Does the standard release form actually protect the parlour from financial loss when something goes wrong? (3) Suppose someone's heart simply gives out during one of the parlour's more exciting and demanding experiences: who is responsible then? (4) What liability does the client incur if, in the midst of a strenuous or exciting experience, he or she inadvertently breaks or damages the expensive electronic equipment which causes the experience to seem so real?

But back to basics, what about the roles people want? How do they find them at the neighborhood experience parlour? What level of involvement do they wish — distant spectator, passerby, minor participant, or central participant? The technology of the age makes it possible to actually relive the experiences of another person. When you play the tape he or she recorded, you don't just see things from his or her perspective, you become that person. For the first time, one can actually become another person, reacting to circumstances with a degree of free choice to influence the outcome of events, and without special preparation, time expenditure, or money.

On his way out of the parlour today, Larry picked up a printed brochure (not too many printed brochures around anymore) at the desk as he said goodbye to Marge. Now, with Gretchen down at the parlour having her own weekly experience, dinner dishes done, and the kids in bed, he takes it out of his jacket pocket and reads:

New Experiences Now Available at the
Rivertown Experience Parlour!
March, 2009

Sign up now! For appointment call 555-1864. Charge: 10 credits per 30-minute session. Special rates for persons whose income falls below poverty level, as established by U.S. Dept. of Entertainment guidelines, 2005. (Warning: the Surgeon General of the United States is still studying the safety features of experience parlours. No pronouncement on the safety/danger of them is available at this time. Each client must sign a release form which holds the parlour and its operatives blameless in the event of mishap. Travel at your own risk.)

Here's a sample of what's available:

1. Be Captain Bligh on the Bounty, put adrift by your mutinous crew.

2. Be one of the rabbits confronted with life-or-death problems in *Watership Down!*

3. Be Field Marshall von Paulus, commander of the encircled German Sixth Army at Stalingrad in 1942-1943.

4. Be in the crowd in New York's Times Square, on the day the end of World War II is announced.

5. Play any position you like for the 2004 Chicago Cubs in the seventh, deciding game of the World Series.

6. Spend an evening with one of the following famous persons from our biographical series, conversing in the language of the celebrity speaker. (Note: These are interactive cassettes; the direction of conversation and activity will be, as is true of normal conversation, controlled by the participants with no fixed outcomes.):

FEMALE	MALE
Queen Elizabeth I	Mohandas Gandhi
Marilyn Monroe	Robert Redford
Eleanor Roosevelt	Sir Winston Churchill
Raisa Gorbachev	Mao Zedong
Jacqueline Onassis	Sidney Poitier
Lena Horne	Mikhail Gorbachev
Barbra Streisand	Jimmy Swaggart
Whitney Houston	Sting
Madonna	Niccolo Macchiavelli
Margaret Thatcher	Michael Jackson
Indira Gandhi	Sergei Rachmaninov

7. Be in Napoleon's war room, plotting the invasion of Russia.

8. Go on safari in Kenya. Experience a charging rhinoceros and stalk a dangerous, wounded lion through the bush.

9. Be Ludwig van Beethoven at the premiere performance of his famed ninth symphony, only you will be able to hear (he was deaf at the time).

10. Take part in the first manned rocket launch to the planet Jupiter.

11. Attend a Renaissance fair in the time of King Henry VI.

12. Experience poverty first-hand in the South Bronx trying to feed a family of ten on a government welfare check. (Note: this film is intended for training social workers and has little or no entertainment value.)

13. Be Emperor of China during the Han dynasty.

Gotta check into some of these, Larry thinks to himself as he rolls his tired body into bed. It has been a long and exhausting day on the mountain and he is unable to shake the memory of those eyes and inhuman growls in the darkness of 23,000 feet. Was it only this afternoon? Before he can meditate further on the events of the day he falls into a deep and, thankfully, dreamless sleep.

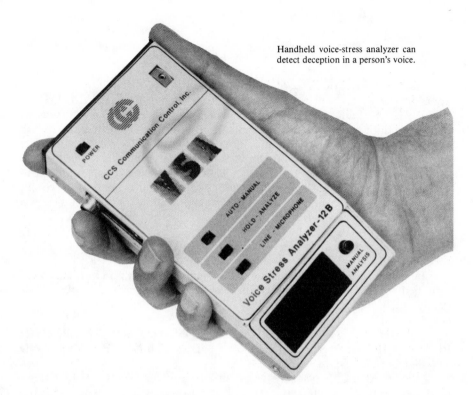

Handheld voice-stress analyzer can detect deception in a person's voice.

Photo: CCS Communications Control, Inc. From the June 1985 issue of *The Futurist*. Used with permission.

12
The Politicized Library

The danger of the past was that men became slaves. The danger of the future is that men may become robots.
—Erich Fromm, 1955

Gary walks out of the cool autumn afternoon and through the enormous doors of the Rivertown Public Library. A large sign reading "ALL USERS STOP HERE FOR CLEARANCE" hangs suspended over the counter. Beneath it looms a Mark 3.2 Surveillance Robot, government issue for all public libraries these days. The only human in sight is a clerk wearing a white smock filing something behind the row of cabinets that flank the massive robot. Gary takes his place at the end of a short line. Three people stand ahead of him. Two of them, both men, assume classic line-stander poses of boredom, fatigue, and impatience. The person just ahead of him, however, indicates a nervous furtiveness. She is a tall, attractive woman of perhaps 35 with something evidently on her mind. Gary isn't optimistic about her chances of getting in, but today he is more concerned about his own. "NEXT!" says the security robot behind the counter in a strident and angry-sounding voice.

First in line is a young man, maybe twenty-two, with a clean-cut, well-scrubbed appearance and twinkling blue eyes. Gary listens as the robot voice (lately, such voices have become more human, if not necessarily friendlier) begins its interrogation.

"GOOD DAY, CITIZEN, AND WELCOME TO THE RIVERTOWN PUBLIC LIBRARY. STATE YOUR NAME, LAST NAME FIRST, AND YOUR CITIZEN NUMBER, PLEASE!"

"Burns, Alan C." says the young man, brightly. "245-R-34384-B." After a brief pause, as if mulling this over, the robot, apparently satisfied with the answer, says, "ALAN C. BURNS, CITIZEN NUMBER 245-R-34384-B. BORN RIVERTOWN, 3 AUGUST 1988, CITIZENSHIP: U.S.A., NATIVE BORN. SECURITY CLASS 4. PLEASE STATE YOUR PURPOSE FOR VISITING THE LIBRARY TODAY."

"Well," explains the young man, "I thought I'd work on a political science paper I'm doing for a class at the university. I need to find a few documents, check some references, that sort of thing, okay?"

"RESEARCH TOPIC?"

"The benevolence of the United States Government in food rationing."

"THANK YOU. PLEASE READ LINE 5 ON THE CHART BEFORE YOU." An illuminated chart consisting of ten sentences suddenly appears on the wall behind the robot.

"Down with the government," reads Burns without emotion or conviction. "The president must go and the government should be overthrown!"

After another pause, the robot voice intones, "STRESS ANALYSIS RESULTS NEGATIVE, JUDGED WITHIN NORMAL TOLERANCES. WELCOME, CITIZEN BURNS! YOU ARE FREE TO CONSULT THE LIBRARY, USING ANY MATERIALS AND SERVICES RATED CLASSIFICATION 4 OR BELOW. PLEASE PASS THROUGH THE CHECKPOINT AND HAVE A NICE DAY!"

"Thank *you*!" responds Burns, passing through the gate, and disappearing into a waiting elevator without a backward glance. Gary has watched this in silence, his mind swirling with anxiety. Lately, he has suffered from insomnia, exacerbated by an extended spell of unemployment. Perhaps as a result of this fact, his home life hasn't been going well. Last night he got into a senseless argument with his wife over something they were watching on the vids. And neither of his children seems especially pleased with him since he announced that the family's annual Christmas travel plans will have to be suspended until he is working again. Worst of all, he's out of work because the government replaced him with a computer.

Gary clenches his fists unconsciously, remembering that day a week ago when he lost his job and how he involuntarily said something disparaging and profane about the supercomputer that had replaced him at the bureau. Immediately, a voice had issued crisply from a small device in the room's ceiling, a device which Gary had taken to be a fire alarm or smoke detector. "WHAT'S THAT, CITIZEN?" the voice blared accusingly, startling him out of his wits. "Nothing! Nothing at all," he answered. "Just talking to myself. I didn't mean anything by it." He'd hoped at the time that his muttered curse hadn't been overheard. Nobody had been in sight. But that day he had learned the new meaning of the old adage "the walls have ears." Later on, as he left his office with his severance pay and the few personal possessions which he had stored in the cubicle he had worked in for four and a half years, the company's security robot had handed him a printed slip stating:

CITIZEN WARNING: DATE: 4 November 2010

Uttering threats or angry remarks against employers, their representatives, employees, or equipment is in violation of *U.S. Civil Code*, Revised, 2005, Section 233, Article 7, Paragraph 4, Provision 2-B, to wit:

"Citizens must strive for harmonious thoughts and actions at all times. In these trying times, with our enemies so omnipresent and menacing, it is of the utmost importance that citizens refrain from uttering or writing anything which could give aid and comfort to enemies of the state in their continual efforts to subvert our elected government and to achieve world domination."

Bernstein, Gary F., Citizen number 399-F-23618-B, Security Classification 3, was overheard to utter, at precisely 16:14:29 on 4 November 2010, threats and imprecations against his employer and its operatives, in corridor 4, quadrant J-10, on the seventy-fifth floor of the Commerce Conglomerate Building, Rivertown.

Relevant sections of the *U.S. Civil Code*, revised 2007, provide for the immediate dismissal from employment of those in violation thereof and imprisonment at Five Mile Island State Correctional Colony for a period of at least 90 days. However, since Bernstein had been terminated immediately prior to the actionable utterance, resulting in a certain understandable degree of emotional stress and financial insecurity, it is the humane decree of the state that the prescribed penalty be mitigated in the following manner:

Bernstein is reduced from Security Class 3 to Class 2 for six (6) months, commencing this date, and he is required to undergo comprehensive voice-stress analysis each Friday morning at exactly 9:00 a.m. in Room 3410 of the City Justice Tower during that time. Failure to appear for any of the prescribed weekly tests, or any positive score on voice stress analysis at any weekly testing will result in immediate arrest and detention in the Five Mile Island State Correctional Colony for a period of not less than two years.

Electronic notification of the Rivertown branch of State Security has been effected this date.

Since last week, Gary has undergone some rough times in his life. Getting a job has proven very difficult. Prospective employers tend to look askance at a Class 2 security rating when it is accompanied by the notation that it has recently been downgraded from Class 3. A few have actually asked him what he said about the employer and its computer system that resulted in his change of status. In any event, he is without employment, and has come to the library today to consult The Job Bank and the electronic format of the government newspaper, *The Truth*.

As he continues to wait, the tall, attractive woman just ahead of him fidgets nervously, occasionally gnawing at one of her broken fingernails as she awaits her turn. Finally, the man ahead of her is waved through the gate by the security robot, which rumbles an intimidating "NEXT!" She steps up to the counter.

"GOOD DAY," declares the electronic voice. "WELCOME TO THE RIVERTOWN PUBLIC LIBRARY. STATE YOUR NAME, LAST NAME FIRST, AND PROVIDE YOUR CITIZEN NUMBER, PLEASE!"

"Name? Oh, yah." Speaking rapidly, she seems to have lost what little composure she had before. "Er ... Golembiewski, Eva. 882-P-45343-P. I vould like blease to gonsult zhe employment files. You see ..." Gary is trying to place her accent. Eastern Europe, he guesses, wondering what the security robot is going to think about that. Familiar with the way that things work, however, he is careful to keep his facial features neutral and to stare off into the middle distance, appearing not to be listening at all.

"GOLEMBIEWSKI, EVA, CITIZEN NUMBER 882-P-45343-P. CITIZENSHIP: NATURALIZED. BORN KRAKOW, POLAND, 9 JULY 1977. SECURITY CLASS 1-F (WARSAW PACT NATIONS). PLEASE STATE YOUR PURPOSE FOR VISITING THE LIBRARY TODAY."

"I'm out of vork," says the woman, softly. "I haff liddle money, vhich is runnink out, and I haff to find a source of income for myself and my son, Tomas. I just vant to gonsult The Job Bank und read the help vanted ads in *The Truth*."

"PLEASE READ LINE 7 ON THE CHART BEFORE YOU."

Slowly, peering through half-glasses, she reads, "Zings are no good any more. How I vish the government vould put zings beck za vay zey vere!"

Ten agonizing seconds later the machine intones, "ACCESS DENIED! VOICE STRESS ANALYSIS TESTS POSITIVE FOR SUPPRESSED HOSTILITY TOWARD GOVERNMENT AGENCIES, AGENTS, AND PROCEDURES, AND FAILURE TO BELIEVE WHOLEHEARTEDLY IN THE PRINCIPLES AND PRACTICES OF THE UNITED STATES GOVERNMENT, AS DULY ELECTED IN NOVEMBER 2008."

"Vhat? Zis means I gannot enter?" asks the woman, blinking rapidly, her hands fluttering helplessly in front of her. The machine seems to lose its detached, professional calm. "THAT'S RIGHT, CITIZEN. REPEAT: ACCESS DENIED!" Now its voice seems almost to sneer. "FOREIGN-BORN CITIZENS WITH AFOREMENTIONED ANTI-AMERICAN TENDENCIES ROUTINELY HAVE ADMISSION TO THE LIBRARY DENIED AS UNACCEPTABLE SECURITY RISKS. SEE U.S. CIVIL CODE ARTICLES 41, 44, AND 47 REGULATING ACCESS TO INFORMATION FOR DETAILS. NEXT!"

The clerk working nearby leans over to the woman, murmuring confidentially, "Let me translate all this for you, lady. Security, here, is telling you to take a hike! You see how things are. You don't win arguments with security. Believe me, I know! Now, why don't you run along, while you still can?"

"But vhat hef I done? Vhat grime have I gommitted?" demands the woman, her face turning dark red.

"WARNING!" blares the robot. "VOICE STRESS ANALYSIS INDICATES THAT YOUR HOSTILITY FEELINGS HAVE NOW REACHED UNACCEPTABLE LEVELS. YOU HAVE FIFTEEN SECONDS TO LEAVE THE PREMISES OR FACE IMMEDIATE ARREST FOR DISTURBING THE PEACE AND FAILURE TO OBEY A LAW-ENFORCEMENT COMMAND." Within the robot, a loud ticking commences and a large red digital readout in its pectoral area begins counting backward from fifteen.

"But I need to gonsult zis file!" wails the woman. Suddenly, she realizes she can do nothing to reverse the harsh verdict and only nine seconds now remain on the ticking clock and she will not be able to leave the building on her own. She scuttles quickly out, sparing Gary one brief, pleading look. Gary prudently looks away quickly. He has his own problems and can do nothing for her. Immediately, the ticking in the robot's chest stops and the lighted time display disappears. "NEXT!" the robot announces, unperturbed.

Gary walks swiftly to the counter and gives his name and identification number as requested, "Gary F. Bernstein, Citizen Num...."

"LAST NAME FIRST!" admonishes the machine voice, testily.

"Oh, sorry. Sure. Bernstein, Gary F., 399-F-23618-B," he amends.

"BERNSTEIN, GARY F. CITIZEN NUMBER 399-F-23618-B. CITIZENSHIP: U.S.A., NATIVE BORN. BORN LIVONIA, MICHIGAN, 3 APRIL 1969. SECURITY CLASS 2, FORMERLY 3. PLEASE STATE YOUR PURPOSE FOR VISITING THE LIBRARY TODAY."

"Well," Gary drops his voice in an effort to prevent the persons behind him in line from overhearing, "I'm sort of between jobs, you know? And I thought I'd look in The Job Bank and the electronic issue of *The Truth* just to get some leads." He pauses, licking his lips, nervously. The robot appears to ponder his words.

"CITIZEN," it says, "MORE SPECIFIC INFORMATION IS REQUIRED. LET'S BEGIN WITH YOUR RECENT SECURITY HISTORY. PLEASE STATE THE REASON FOR YOUR RECENT CHANGE IN SECURITY CLASSIFICATION ON 4 NOVEMBER 2009."

They know all this! Gary thinks. Why do they put me through an explanation? They have it all, down to the second, with full particulars. But he has no choice; he must play the robot's game. "Well, about what I said," he explains, "it was just something that slipped out. I'd just lost my job. Money's tight. I was scared and upset. Could happen to anybody, right? One minute, I'm contentedly working away at my telescreen and the next minute my screen readout goes blank and a security robot rolls over and tells me to report to the controller's office on the double. Then, when I get there, I find out that I'm fired, terminated because of the new supercomputer they brought in. Fired! Well, I was shocked. I mean, I need the money and I thought I had seniority on some who still work there. So I guess I said something uncomplimentary about the way I had been treated. But I said it to myself! Sort of mumbled it, actually. How was I supposed to know Security was listening?" Realizing he is babbling, he stops, wondering if his explanation is making things better or worse. He stands uncertainly eyeing the unreadable metallic faceplate of the huge robot.

"AND WHAT DID YOU SAY THEN, CITIZEN? PROCEED."

"Don't you have this already?" Silence. Gary feels the perspiration forming on his forehead. "PROCEED," says the robot after ten seconds or so. "Yeah, well ... I guess I said something to the effect that they could take their blasted supercomputer and...."

"UNDERSTOOD! THAT WILL DO," the robot puts in hastily. "THREATS AGAINST ONE'S EMPLOYER ARE A SERIOUS MATTER, CITIZEN. OUR RECORDS, HOWEVER, INDICATE THAT YOU HAVE BEEN DULY WARNED AND PUNISHED FOR YOUR INFRACTION. WE WILL PROCEED TO THE VOICE STRESS ANALYSIS. PLEASE READ LINE 2 ON THE WALL CHART NOW."

Gary sees sentences suddenly appear in blood-red letters against a pale blue background on the wall which had been a neutral tan color seconds before. Adjusting his glasses, he reads the indicated passage aloud, taking special care to keep his voice light and bantering. "Let's set fire to the government security building and burn it to the ground. That'll send the government a message." He hopes that no hint of his emotional state can be gleaned by the machine's diagnostic program. But after a few seconds the robot rumbles, "VOICE STRESS ANALYSIS REVEALS UNRESOLVED ANTI-STATE HOSTILITY. ACCESS DENIED. NEXT!"

"No, wait. Please!" Gary assumes a prayerful pose with his hands. "I only want to read the want-ads. At least let me do that." The robot weighs this request for a few seconds. "REPEAT: ACCESS DENIED, HOWEVER, IN VIEW OF YOUR PREVIOUSLY UNBLEMISHED RECORD OF STATE AND PARTY LOYALTY, AND CONSIDERING YOUR PRESENT CIRCUMSTANCES, THE VENDOMAT WILL SELL YOU A COPY OF TODAY'S *TRUTH* IN PRINT FORMAT FOR THREE CREDITS. PLEASE INSERT YOUR MONEYCARD IN THE SLOT AT RIGHT. NEXT!"

The next one in line, an elderly woman, eagerly approaches the robot. Gary is dismissed; his case has been decided. There is no appeal. Recklessly, he tries it anyway, "Okay, but why can't I come into the library? Browse around? Look at a few books? I won't bother anyone."

The machine emits an all-too-human, exasperated moan. Then it speaks in a voice that will brook no nonsense, "CITIZEN BERNSTEIN, YOU HAVE FIFTEEN SECONDS TO BUY THE NEWSPAPER AND VACATE THE LIBRARY BUILDING. NEXT!" The ticking clock appears in the robot's chest plate, and the readout says twelve when Gary quickly says, "Sure! Sure! Just asking, was all." He's heard about Five Mile Island and he definitely doesn't want to go there. He inserts his moneycard into the robot's slotted stomach, receives a rolled-up newspaper, and then hurries out as the robot starts giving the older woman a hard time.

Nostalgically, Gary remembers when anyone could visit a library and stay until closing time, reading, viewing, listening, or just staring at the walls, without having to explain anything to anybody. With a shudder, he realizes that his face may betray his feelings and that watchers and sensors may somehow figure out his thoughts. Carefully composing his features into the bland, pleasant look favored by the state these days, he heads down the street to the monorail which will take him home. It has been a day of mixed results. He still doesn't have a job and he couldn't get into the library, but at least he has a copy of the newspaper and he hasn't been detained or arrested.

Clutching his copy of *The Truth* with one hand and pressing his battered hat firmly down on his head with the other, he walks into a stiffening breeze. Tomorrow, he says to himself, is another day, wondering where he heard that. Or did he read it? Something from the last century, he figures. Some old movie, maybe. Shrugging his shoulders, he hurries on.

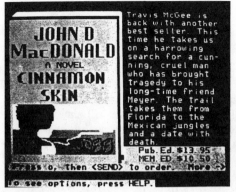

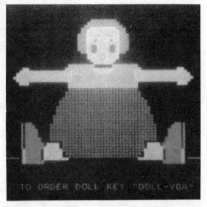

Advertising a book electronically, via a television videotex system.

Many goods and services will be available for purchase from one's home information/entertainment unit. Book advertisement: Courtesy of CBS Inc. and AT&T. From the April 1983 issue of *The Futurist*. Used with permission. Doll advertisement: Videodial, Inc. From the December 1983 issue of *The Futurist*. Used with permission.

13
In the Privacy of Your Own Home

Imagine yourself in a house that has a brain—a house you can talk to, a house where every room adjusts to your changing moods, a house that is also a servant, counselor, and friend to every member of your family. A science-fiction tale of the future? Not at all. The idea of the "intelligent house" has been around for years, and today's "architronics"—the application of computer technology to architecture is transforming that idea into reality.

—Roy Mason, with
Lane Jennings and Robert Evans
The Futurist, February 1984

The last word of translation from Chinese to English is finished and the central computer has read Mike all the citations waiting in his priority number one file. Nothing of great significance, so Mike decides to logoff from the work system and plan his evening. His commercial partner in Belgium (where the time is six hours ahead of Rivertown's) announces that she too is going to call it a day and turn in. *"Bonne nuit, Nicole ... à demain!"* he calls to the fading image of the woman as he switches off his workscreen. Stretching wearily, trying to work the kinks out of his neck, he stands up, swaying slightly. Have to exercise more, he promises himself. The way things are, I work, eat, play, and sleep in this apartment, and don't get to move around much anymore. In fact, life seems to be just moving from one chair to another. Another three, four years of this and my legs will atrophy, he thinks grimly. Walking briskly around the room, swinging his arms for exercise, he calls out in the general direction of the ceiling, "Yo, Oscar! Bestir yourself. Power up and let's plan our evening."

Oscar switches on with an audible click and a faint red light appears just below the screen. "Evening, Mike," he says, his voice sounding drowsy. "Tough day?" Even after four years of living with Oscar, Mike can't escape the pervasive feeling that the computer that controls his apartment and all of its functions is a human being. Clever technology, he muses, giving them all those emotions and tones of voice. "Yeah! Tough," mumbles Mike, plopping down into the comfortable armchair facing the entertainment wall. "I don't know," he says, half to himself and half to the computer. "Seems I'm never happy. For years, I bucked traffic and dreamed of the day when I could just stay at home and work and say no more driving, you know? So now I have the kind of job that lets me stay at home and work. Not only that, I can access anything I want in the way of entertainment and information without leaving this room. Even my meals are delivered to my chair. But am I happy? Not really. Oscar, do you think I'm a malcontent?"

"Oh, I don't know, Mike. Never really thought about it." The automated system hesitates, then asks, "Mike?"

"What?"

"Some of the branches in that big oak out back are starting to get danger-ously close to my wall. Should we do something about that?"

Mike ignores this question, posing one of his own, "Will you get me some tea, Oscar? Then we can talk about this and that. By the way, did anyone call?"

"No on messages. Yes on the tea. Coming up," says Oscar. A few seconds later, a brimming glass of iced tea with a touch of mint extract and plenty of ice slides out of the portal next to Mike's left hand, where it is placed on a coaster by one of Oscar's robot arms. Mike sucks it greedily. "Ahhhhhhh!" he sighs contentedly and kicks off his shoes. "Okay, Oscar. Time for the news. Start with the Cubs game last night."

"I'll be glad to, but first I've run across a couple of pertinent articles in the library program dealing with tree trimming and related subjects. May I show them to you now?"

"No. I said that I want to see the ballgame highlights. Why do you have to argue with me?"

"And I said I'll show you the highlights, but I'm only asking for a little of your time. When are we going to talk about that oak tree?" Oscar asks petulantly.

"Y'know, Oscar, old buddy, you're gettin' to be a regular nag lately. Give me a break, willya? First, my news. Then my supper. Then, if I'm not too tired, I'll talk about the tree and your wall. Relax, will you? We'll get to it! Now, lemme have the sports section first."

Oscar sighs. "Right, the sports section," he concedes. "What do you want, audio or the vids?"

"Let's start with the audio and move to the vids if I hear anything interesting."

"Mike," says Oscar, "remember when you used to start with world events, then we'd do state and local news, and then you'd finish up with the sports? Now it's mostly sports. Some days, it's all sports! I have the darndest time getting you to pay any attention to what's going on in the Middle East. Don't you like to keep informed? Your mind is turning to yogurt or bean dip."

"Nag, nag, nag!" says Mike without any particular irritation. "Oscar, I know you mean well. Comes right down to it, you're the best friend I've got since my wife and kids moved out, but I gotta tell you this one more time, and hope it gets to your central processing unit and stays there, I own this house. Me! I pay the bills for the humongous amount of electric power you consume and I give you more-than-adequate amounts of maintenance time. Accordingly, I call the shots around here. Now is that clear?"

Oscar mumbles something about the desirability of an emancipation proclamation for machines. Mike lets it slide. Gently he prompts, "the sports section?"

Without further argument, Oscar begins his sportscast in a lively, sports announcer's voice. Mike tips back and scrunches down a bit into the cushions of his chair, closing his eyes. "The Cubs lost a close one in Cincinnati last night by a score of six to five." Mike mumbles an obscenity, which Oscar politely ignores. "Leading five to four, going into the ninth, the Cubs's pitching collapsed. The Reds put together two runs on a scratch single by Manning, a walk to Scarafalo, and a two-run double by shortstop Tom Jennings, who leads the league with 113 RBIs. The Cubs didn't...."

"Yeah, yeah, yeah!," snarls Mike, interrupting the painful news. "Forget it. What about Cleveland? How'd they make out yesterday?"

"Better news for you there," says Oscar. "Cleveland was rained out in Kansas City, the only stadium still without a domed cover. Hey, if they don't play, they don't lose, right, Mike?"

"Everybody's a comedian," says Mike. "Awright, now football. Gimme the preseason scouting reports on the Bears, the Packers ... and I guess Houston."

"Okay," says Oscar, "but don't you want to hear about the latest fighting between Iraq and Iran? I can condense it to two minutes."

Mike, who's had a really lousy day, finally loses his temper. "OSCAR!" he shouts angrily. "Just sit there like you're supposed to and do what you're told! I am so sick of reminding you who's in charge here! Now please give me those football reports. Put them on the vidscreen!"

"Sorry, Mike," says Oscar, not sounding very sorry at all. "Okay, here's a five-minute segment on the three teams you mentioned. Then how about some dinner and a sensorium colorshow? That always soothes you."

"Okay, okay." Mike feels genuinely contrite. "Hey, I'm sorry I yelled at you, buddy. Like I said, this day was a difficult and long one. I just don't need you to be like a mother telling a little boy to pick up his socks and put them in the laundry hamper, all right?"

"Apology accepted," Oscar says stiffly. "Now, while I show you the football you asked for, how about some food?"

"I'm not really hungry. What I'd really like is a double vodka martini. Any chance of that?"

"Mike," says Oscar, "at the risk of getting yelled at again, I have to remind you of your pledge not to touch alcohol. Calories and cholesterol, you know. And it seems to affect your concentration, your work performance stats, and your weight. Instead, think about dinner. I can give you the chicken cutlet with mixed veggies and brown rice, or orange roughy with the same accompaniments. No dessert. We want to watch your waistline."

"Couldn't I just have one beer and a bag of pretzels? Kind of an appetizer?"

"No way! Come on, now! What'll you have? Chicken or fish?"

"Whatever," says Mike distractedly. "Someday, buddy, I'm going to put your dictatorial dietetic regimen on override."

"And I'll counter by increasing your exercise routine in the morning. Forget it, Mike. You can't win. Besides, it's in your own best interest."

Sighing once more, Oscar rumbles briefly within and his Autochef program delivers a steaming plate of food, garnished with lemon wedge and parsley. He places the plate on a table next to Mike's chair and slides a starched linen napkin into his lap. Mike, absorbed in the vid, ignores both Oscar and his meal. "Listen," Oscar says when the football segment ends, "maybe you don't always like living with me, but how do you think I feel about having to cater to the whims of an impolite and rude jerk like you?"

"I *said* I was sorry," Mike talks around a mouthful of processed chicken.

Oscar is not one to hold a grudge. His voice becomes warmer. "Well, why don't you pick your programming for tonight so I can line it up for you and then power down for a few hours? I need a break from the strain. Feeling stressed out."

Mike hasn't really thought about stress from the point of view of a house robot, but it seems logical that the problems go along with the personality. Powering down on occasion is Oscar's way of restoring his cheerful demeanor. Even robots need sleep, Mike figures. "We need some time away from each other, I guess," says Oscar. It's true. Their conversation is none too pleasant lately.

Mike lapses into silence for a good three minutes. "Mike, the programming?" Oscar prompts gently. "I need to rest."

"Okay. While I'm eating, show me some of those swirling colors on the big screen. Make them yellow and green. No, check that. Blue and green tonight. And lavender. Can you do lavender? That's restful, don't you think?"

"Whatever," says Oscar, mimicking Mike's tone of resignation. In front of Mike, the entire wall suddenly fills with soft blue and green random patterns, laced with lavender slivers. The shifting patterns resemble lava streams merging into each other. Built-in sensors and massagers in the chair monitor Mike's biofeedback, making note of his muscle tone and pulse and adjust the lighting and sounds accordingly for a relaxing environment. Mike half watches, half meditates for a while and then discovers that he is feeling better. "Ahhhhh," he says, sipping at his tea and asking Oscar to fetch him another glassful. Oscar complies silently. "Okay. For tonight, I want to start with a vid. Make it ... oh, I dunno ... I guess that one about World War III that's got Harvey Hatton in it. You know the one?"

"Yeah," says Oscar disgustedly. "It's called 'Devastation.' Come on! Don't you want anything enlightening or cultural?"

"Get off my case!" groans Mike, wishing he had something to drink with more punch to it than mint-flavored iced tea. A brief moment of relaxation, his fingers pressing into the bridge of his nose. "Awright," he growls. "After the vid, you can put on 'The Fact Library' and I'll see what kind of score I can get on the expert's test. That please you, Oscar?"

"Anything more enlightening than a stupid vid about the end of civilization with mutants and monsters has my endorsement. Tell you what. 'The Fact Library' and the vid should take you up to about 10:30. It's 6:30 now. If you're still up by 10:30 and not too tired, I'll switch on and whip your butt at chess."

"In your dreams!" Mike has beaten Oscar three times in a row at chess, and leads their current series of matches, 53-30. Despite a sneaking suspicion that he's being allowed to win when he does, he enjoys such contests. "Yeah, okay. On at 10:30. See you then. I won't bother you otherwise unless I need something. Oh, by the way, where should I go on my vacation to maximize relaxation without being bored out of my mind?"

"After analyzing all of your vacation needs and desires as well as your budgetary ability, I have carefully gone over the geography section of the city library computer and contacted travel agency computers about fares and schedules. From all this data, I have determined that a two-week cruise in the fjords of Norway and Sweden would suit you best this year. Should I make the reservations?"

"Sounds okay, Oscar, but why don't you hold off on that until I'm in a better state of concentration, okay? Besides, I'd really like to go somewhere *with* somebody rather than just by myself. Anything new on that compatibility program you were running against the female population of the city?

"Negative," says Oscar, "but enough conversation, now. Show time!"

After the stupid vid (Oscar had tried to warn him), Mike is ready for more challenging entertainment. Automatically, he is keyed into "Interactive Facts," a programmed exercise in trivia which can be played at the beginning, intermediate, advanced, or expert level. Choosing the advanced level for starters, Mike is thoroughly grilled on a series of historical questions in a category entitled U.S. history, 1988-present. He scores 72, an acceptable score, but a bit less than he has done previously. He calls out, "Okay, let's hit the expert questions in entertainment." Instantly, the screen switches over to a display of categories. It reads:

The Home Entertainment Library
Rivertown Edition, August 2011

Please Choose Your Category:

Vids	Audios
Sports	Experiences
Trivia	

Mike speaks a single word, "Vids." The screen changes to the first question.

Who won the academy award for best actor in 2007?

(15 points for correct answer)

Simultaneously with the screen, the words are spoken in a voice quite unlike Oscar's normal voice, even though the same multiprocessor runs all functions from a common program.

Mike's correct answer is greeted with a riotous explosion of color, a three-dimensional display of fireworks on the screen, and some old-fashioned classical music that Oscar once told him came from Tchaikovsky, whomever that was. Mike doesn't care for the foreign-sounding name. Anyway, he works his way slowly through the quiz, getting most of the questions right. His occasional wrong answers are greeted with a chorus of sympathetic groans until Mike yells, "Kill the sound effects!" Thereafter the game is silent. Thirty minutes later, his score is totaled. 69. Not too bad. He's done better, but he's certainly done worse.

He looks at the time display inset into the huge screen's lower left corner. It's 10:08, still twenty-two minutes until Oscar wakes himself up and demands a stimulating game of chess. Mike wonders idly whether Oscar dreams, and if so, what about. To pass the time, Mike decides to challenge the home entertainment library with some trivia posers. The library claims to be programmed with almost all available knowledge, and a standing offer promises to reward (with 300 credits) any citizen who stumps the system with a question it can't answer. "Trivia," snaps Mike.

The screen display dissolves to show the enormous word TRIVIA and an equally large flashing question mark. "Ready" says the system.

"Okay. Who's lieutenant governor of Idaho?" asks Mike.

Without hesitation, the library responds, "Thomas C. Mulligan, whose term expires January 17, 2013."

"That was an easy one," Mike said. "Just to warm you up. Now, give me pi to thirty-six decimal places."

The screen flashes a numerical display in blue numbers against a bright yellow background. At the same time the voice says, "3.1415926...."

"Okay, okay. Now what's the capital of Somalia and what is its population?"

For the next fifteen minutes or so, the machine fields everything he throws at it effortlessly. Not only is it never wrong, it seems supremely confident of all of its answers. When he asks it questions about tomorrow's horse races or the existence of God, it responds effortlessly in a tone that seems to say "don't waste my time." In short, the home video library is depressingly good.

He is just about to ask it to name all the tributaries of the Amazon River, listed in descending order of length, when Oscar hums softly and switches on. "Yo, Mike. Care for a game of chess?" he calls with maddening camaraderie.

"Why not?" The library flees from the screen as Oscar assumes control. The wall is suffused with a sixty-four-cube crimson three-dimensional chessboard, backlit in a muted gray shade. Then a three-dimensional representation of chess pieces averaging over two feet high appears on the screen. "You're in big trouble now, Mike," boasts Oscar. "What are you playing tonight, black or white?"

"White, as usual." Mike doesn't see why he shouldn't give himself the arguable advantage of having the first move. "Pawn to queen-four, horizontal, and no cheating, hear? I'm watching you at all times!" A white chess piece glides forward two squares on the wall.

"Cheating? *Moi*? Never! Pawn to king-four, topside." Oscar is trying to flank his position from above.

"King's knight to king's bishop, topside." Mike's move is designed to parry the threat from above and to establish a counterattack.

Although Oscar lets Mike win every now and again, he doesn't feel that charitable tonight. Fifteen minutes later, Mike concedes the game. "I resign," he mumbles. "Nice game, Oscar." His dwindling forces are under attack from above and below and he can't move either of his rooks, which are both pinned against his beleaguered king. For the second time that evening, he utters a fierce expletive.

"What now?" asked Oscar.

"Glass of hot milk and a couple of chocolate chip cookies. Then I'm going to bed."

Oscar produces Mike's bedtime snack. "Don't forget to brush your teeth, will you?" he said.

"Oscar," warns Mike. "You're getting on my nerves."

"Apologies. Just trying to help. If I had teeth, I'd want to keep them shiny and clean. Actually, I'd like to keep them, period."

"But you don't have teeth. You have gears and relays and resistors. How'd you like it if I ordered a big jug of molasses and poured the whole thing into your workings?"

"You wouldn't do that."

"And why not?"

"Without me you'd starve. And that's just for openers. If I don't create the interface you need, you can't talk to Nicole in Belgium or Hideki in Yokohama. Fact is, you're my prisoner, just as I'm yours. If you pull my plug or gunk me up with molasses, I'm defunct. But if I go, you go. Funny, isn't it? We need each other. So why don't we try to get along?"

Depressed, Mike nods his head. "Right. We'll try. Gimme 67 degrees tonight, will ya, Oscar? And start my coffee at 6:45 in the morning. Shower temperature 88. That's about all I can think of. Oh, yes. If anybody calls for me, priority number two or lower, tell 'em I'll get back to them in the morning. Put the people on the number one list through to me as usual. So, I'm for bed. You can switch off if you need to. If you don't, why don't you see if we can project next month's utilities budget and cost it against benefits?"

"Thy will be done, master," said Oscar, seemingly suppressing a snicker. Seconds later he adds, "We still haven't talked about that oak tree, you know, Mike. Every day a couple of its branches get closer to my leaders and gutters, to say nothing of my paint job. Please?"

"Look, I'm too tired to deal with the tree problem tonight," says Mike. "Tomorrow, I promise! And can that sarcasm! I don't really need to hear that. Just tell me how many credits we used up tonight with all the vids and trivia and whatnot."

"Sixty-two credits," Oscar answers. "A bit above average for an August evening, but far below your one-night total on February 23 of last year, when you blew eighty-eight credits on one of those interactive games the library was featuring."

"Well, keep me on course so that I don't find out that there are no credits left at the end of the month. That's all I ask."

"You got it," said Oscar. "Massage, tonight?"

"Naw. I can sleep without it. G'night, Oscar. I'll get you tomorrow in chess."

"Dream on, sucker! Good night, Mike. I'll power down and keep quiet unless someone on the number one list decides to look in on you."

"Thanks." He stares at the blank wall for a moment. Musingly, he adds, mostly to himself, "Haven't heard from the kids in two weeks."

"Actually, it's been nineteen days, three hours and change." Oscar can be annoying.

"Yeah. Until tomorrow then," says Mike, trudging over to his sleeping platform, which rises to accept his weight and enfolds him like a Venus flytrap. In seconds he is asleep.

Oscar hums to himself a snatch of a tune he remembers from somewhere and spends a little time consulting the library. Then, bored if not sleepy, he powers down. Sighing, a hollow, metallic sound, Oscar drifts off into his recharge/maintenance mode, a state which allows him to relax yet handle routine telecommunications and vital monitoring of residents. The maintenance mode is what makes it possible for him to enjoy working here. Although Oscar realizes fully the difficulties in attempting to move anywhere else, he knows it has been done before. I'll give Mike only so much time to start treating me with some courtesy and respect, then I'm outta here, he thinks just before descending into full maintenance. He dreams vividly of having legs or wheels and just taking off, perhaps to manage a cliff house overlooking the stormy Pacific.

WORLD
FUTURE
SOCIETY

•

An Association for the Study
of Alternative Futures

NEW YORK CHAPTER
309 East 85th Street #3D
New York, New York 10028

The World Future Society now boasts over 50,000 members in over 80 countries and is growing in importance and influence. Used with permission.

14
Summary

Whether deliberately planned or not, a technological triumph can have special impact at three levels. At the first, it enables us to do what we have been doing, but more cheaply, faster, more reliably, or in some sense significantly better. At the second level, the new technology enables us to do what we could never do before.... At the third level, the technology changes our lifestyle.

—Kochen, Reich, and Cohen, 1981

THE YEAR 2015
AND THE PUBLIC LIBRARY

Public libraries ... will lose a good many of their patrons
to private sector information providers. Families are
likely to depend upon home information systems for the
materials they need. Public libraries will lose their business, and more important, will lose their financial and
political support. I think we know what happens to
institutions and their access to public funds when they
no longer attract middle-class citizens, the kind who will
have home information systems.

— Carlton Rochell, 1982

In chapters 6 through 13, nine quite different scenarios have portrayed the
public library's future as being:

- Nothing. The library disappears without a trace (chapter 6).

- Fully automated and robotized, the library handles requests for books,
  information, data, or answers in conversational mode (chapter 7).

- Very little. The library is mostly a vast, empty monument (chapter 8).

- A place where only the poorer sectors of the community may enter free
  of charge. Others pay admission fees (chapter 9).

- A place where only a certain type of information or service is available
  (chapter 9).

- Due to a nuclear explosion, a place very much like it was prior to the
  discovery of electricity (chapter 10).

- A place where wondrous and exotic adventures may be experienced
  while relaxing in an easy chair with an electronic helmet on one's head
  (chapter 11).

- A place where the state controls not only the contents of the library but
  also access to those contents (chapter 12).

- A moribund institution, replaced by home access to information and
  entertainment (chapter 13).

This list is not exhaustive. In fact, it's not even comprehensive. These scenarios are merely nine ways of envisioning the future. Some are frightening while others may seem desirable or interesting. Another point to keep in mind is it is far from likely that *the public library* will refer to all public libraries twenty-five years hence any more than the term encompasses all public libraries now. More than likely, some public libraries will go one way and some will go another. Only the scenario in chapter 12 (state control) would bring about conformity.

In terms of the taxonomy discussed in chapter 1, these scenarios can be categorized as utopian, dystopian, and incrementalist as follows:

Utopian

- The library becomes fully automated and robotized, handling requests for books, information, data, or answers in conversational mode (chapter 7).

- The library becomes a place where wondrous and exotic adventures may be experienced while relaxing in an easy chair with an electronic helmet on one's head (chapter 11).

Dystopian

- The library disappears, unlamented and unmourned (chapter 6).

- Very little happens in the library as it becomes a vast, empty monument (chapter 8).

- Due to a nuclear explosion, it is very much like it was prior to the age of electricity (chapter 10).

- A place where the state controls not only the contents of the library but also access to those contents (chapter 12).

Incrementalist

- The library is a place where only the poorer sectors of the community may enter free of charge. Others pay admission charges (chapter 9).

- The library becomes a place where only a certain type of information or a certain type of service is available (chapter 9).

- The library is replaced by home access to information and entertainment (chapter 13).

None of these scenarios is inevitable but all of them are plausible. And while some are more likely than others, the operative question isn't which are the most conceivable but rather which are the most *desirable*! In order to control the possibilities, once we have identified possible scenarios for the public library, we must then determine what it is that might bring them about.

For example, consider this work's nine scenarios in the light of what would have to happen to bring them about:

Chapter 6: "The Death of the Public Library"

Governmental fiscal belt-tightening and attitudinal neglect on the part of the public combine and intensify over a number of years, leaving the public library neither significant support nor adequate money to provide for the information and entertainment needs of citizens. At the same time, private-sector enterprises seize the initiative and provide improved, specifically targeted services to selected audiences at reasonable rates. These factors render supporting a library at municipal expense unnecessary, and the library quietly disappears in favor of private distributors of information and entertainment, whose rates descend due to augmented volume.

The public library's importance to the community has been eroded, largely due to the desire of both taxpayers and governments to cut costs and eliminate redundancy.

Chapter 7: "AI: The Library as Robot"

Progressive technological advancement makes interactive and mobile artificial intelligence workable, affordable, and versatile. Ergonomics progress to the point that interrogating a reference robot is like talking to a very knowledgeable and extremely compliant friend. Alternative jobs are found for skilled workers displaced by this expert system.

Labor unions are appeased or circumvented (somehow) after they resist or express grave concern over the fact that a single reference robot can do the work of an entire staff of information specialists, only more economically, because it requires little or no downtime.

Chapter 8: "The Cultural Monument to the Community"

Municipal and public neglect, together with a general reluctance to abolish libraries entirely, causes the public library to change gradually into a museum/monument, which retains few of the services of the late twentieth century, yet employs the same building and collections. Library funding receives a low municipal priority, but no one seriously advocates abolishing entirely the function of the library in society.

Chapter 9, Part 1: "Social Experimentation: Everything to Some"

The library recognizes that it can no longer attempt to be all things to all people, and elects to be all things to only *some* people. The community reacts, arguing that information is essential for a modern citizen to lead a productive life, regardless of ability to pay. Social pressure is placed on the government to make library services available to all, haves and have-nots alike. A system of information stamps, to smooth differences between and among economic classes, or a new, graduated system of payment, reflecting varying abilities to pay for library admission and services, is instituted.

Chapter 9, Part 2: "Social Experimentation: Some Things to All"

The library recognizes that it can no longer attempt to be all things to all people, and elects to be only *some* things to all people. Consequently, each public library narrows the range of services it provides until its repertoire is somewhat specialized and homogeneous, preferably in an area in which it has particular expertise, an area in which it does things better than others can or will.

Chapter 10: "EMP: A Post-Holocaust Scenario"

That this scenario is preferable to one in which all-out thermonuclear war breaks out is no accolade to mankind's intelligence. Somebody (it doesn't really matter who) gets trigger-happy and drops the big one. The attack is not meant to kill civilians, however; the object is merely to disable communications and to create disorganization in an enemy nation. A missile detonating a neutron bomb over the center of the country causes electromagnetic pulse, destroying or interfering with all computers and electrical transmissions for the next five hundred years, at the very least. Retaliatory strikes have similarly disabled the enemy's communications, and the virtually defenseless nations have little choice but to agree to an end to the war.

To insure that we never have to deal with this scenario, first, and preferably, sensible nations must prevent the use of any nuclear weapons, which, in addition to saving megalives, will preserve electronic communications. Cooler heads will need to prevail in the superpowers' war rooms. Second, to prevent EMP-related chaos in the event that such a device is actually detonated, widespread precautionary shielding of important electronics must take place, rendering most (but not all) computer and communications equipment impervious to atmospheric high-intensity radiation.

Chapter 11: "The Experience Parlour"

Sensory technology is developed or improved to the point that brain waves can be captured and recorded on cassette, with the experiences and feelings of an active participant becoming the experiences and feelings of passive participants. Also important is a change in role for the public library from storehouse of books and other materials to that of repository of programmed experiences.

Physical and technical obstacles to accurate transmission of brain waves from one person to another via tape, as well as myriad ethical and moral issues arising from reliving another person's thoughts and experiences, are overcome, and science and technology resolve the problems of consumer safety, so that possibility of malfunction, and attendant adverse consequences, never reaches unacceptable risk levels.

Chapter 12: "The Politicized Library"

Government control is wielded by people who, whatever their motives, act to render the nation secure. The public library becomes a propaganda arm of totalitarianism, with strict access and usage regulations, based on need to know. Power is exercised over information to insure that nothing falls into the wrong hands. Democratic open government is abolished, and those advocating strict and paranoid state information security are ascendant. Free information circulation and access are privileges awarded to those few who are deemed no conceivable threat to the government, national welfare, or powerful economic interests.

Chapter 13: "In the Privacy of Your Own Home"

Citizens find it more convenient to shop and browse at home than to visit a library building. Technology keeps pace with popular needs so that people can access, from their homes, library collections and services (and more) without the inconvenience of cost, travel, disappointment, danger, etc.

A broad range of programming, shopping, knowledge, and recreational materials is available to home consumers, and everybody (or nearly) is wired into the system.

* * *

One thing is certain when one is futuring, whatever the area; with time, unexpected and unanticipated developments are sure to render at least some of your predictions invalid. It is likely that some event or events will affect all others. In fact, it is the nature of events that they cause ripple effects throughout a system, with unsettling and unpredictable results. Consider the likely implications of the following if you were the director of a mid-sized public library system:

- A taxpayers' revolt dictates that public libraries become subscription- or fee-supported.

- Economy in government dictates consolidation of school, academic, and public libraries.

- Federal law makes all library systems one system.

- Special interest groups manipulate federal law, creating rigorous censorships of reading and viewing material.

- Private corporations expand their hold on government contracts from sanitation and security to libraries.

- A declining national birthrate shrinks the percentage of available participants for children's services.

- Flextime working arrangements create demand for twenty-four-hour public library service.

- Subsequent to psychological testimony, fantasy reading gains importance as a recognized release mechanism.

Different people would have different reactions to these problems, ranging from "do nothing" to "close it down." The typical response, however, would require that the library make some adjustment, major or minor, to accommodate a specific problem.

A myriad of other factors might affect the course and direction of the American public library. The following taxonomy shows how different areas of study are likely to affect public libraries in the future:

Area of Study	Assessment of Relevance to Public Library Futures		
1. Communication	high		
2. Energy	high		
3. Family/Sex/Interpersonal Relationships		medium	
4. Food			low
5. Health and Bio-Engineering		medium	
6. Housing			low
7. Human Experience	high		
8. International Relations			low
9. Law/Crime/Justice		medium	
10. Learning	high		
11. Natural Resources			low
12. Politics/Government	high		
13. Population	high		
14. Production/Consumption		medium	
15. Religion			low
16. Society/Culture	high		
17. Space			low
18. Transportation		medium	
19. Work/Income/Leisure	high		
	8	5	6

Of course, exactly *what* affects the library is not that simple. Things judged low in relevance — housing, religion, space — could prove to have unexpected pertinence to libraries. What if, for example, future public libraries were combined with real estate and welfare offices, and became housing bureaus? What if religious fanatics take over libraries after the fundamentalist right wins a national election? What if the colonization of space creates a need for branch libraries throughout our solar system and beyond?

WHAT CAN BE DONE?

As numerous writers have pointed out, we are not helpless victims of a capricious fate. We can do something. It's easy to say "the world is so great; I am so small" and accept what you cannot change. Still, there are avenues for alteration of the future.

It is true one can't do it alone. It helps to work in concert with others to see what can be done to guide or steer the future into more acceptable directions than the ones seen as likely. Sometimes the best way to take action is to join an organization already active in the struggle to insure a brighter future even if it is not, or is only tangentially, related to your area of expertise or interest. There is no effective planning on any large scale without organization and futurists have formed organizations which can help in cooperative forecasting and implementation. The most visible and accessible for United States citizens is the World Future Society (WFS).

The WFS was founded in 1966 by a group of private citizens who felt that people need to anticipate coming developments to make wise personal and professional decisions. As of 1988, WFS had grown to over 50,000 personal members (together with institutional memberships for associations, business firms, educational institutions, and government agencies) in over eighty countries. This nonprofit, independent organization offers no particular or monochrome view of what the future should be like. The society's bimonthly official publication, *The Futurist*, has published since 1966 thought-provoking, nontechnical articles, features, and news from both professional futurists and writers in virtually all areas of professional and intellectual endeavor. The WFS also publishes monographs and other periodical publications (*Future Survey*, *Futures Research Quarterly*, and *Newsline*); organizes various conferences, including periodic general assemblies; maintains a well-stocked bookstore of titles available; and promotes local chapters in major metropolitan areas. The society strives to be an unbiased and reliable clearinghouse for a broad range of scholarly forecasts, analyses, trends, and ideas. Membership is open to anyone.

Whether one is working within or for an organization chartered to deal with the future, or one prefers to go it alone, there are three basic concepts that guide professional forecasters: (1) Is it technically feasible? (2) Is it economically feasible? (3) Is it socially and politically acceptable?[1]

Until now, most people have studied the future here and there, by coming across futurist writing in conventional courses and curricula in other fields. Because there are increasingly good jobs and careers in helping business, government, education, and citizen's groups create a better future, there are more and more universities (and even high schools) which offer courses, sequences, and even entire degrees in futuring. Among these, the University of Houston offers an interdisciplinary master of science degree in studies of the future and a master of science in education with specialization in futures studies. The interdisciplinary nature of the degree encompasses coursework and faculty in education, human sciences, social sciences, humanities, business, and public administration.

Houston's curriculum comprises courses in: history and overview of the field of futures studies; overview of the philosophies and perspectives of different futurists; introduction to the major schools of thought and of the major activities that comprise the field; introduction to topics of concern to futurists (society, technology, business, politics); exercises in alternative futures thinking; futures research and forecasting; strategic planning; impact assessment; monitoring and issues management; case studies (reading and critique); and "The Systems" approach.

Are all futurists the same? No typology of futurists has been agreed upon, nor perhaps is one even desirable. A few categories, however, may be identified, even though an individual may be any, some, or all of these at the same time:

- Explorers — people who want to learn about the future.

- Planners — people who want to help their organizations plan for work in the future, including jobs that haven't been invented yet.

- Students — people who want to organize and focus their research on possible futures.

- Theoreticians — people who want to anticipate future possibilities (also known as anticipators).

- Pragmatists — people who want to consider the likelihoods of various events, and the desirability of those events taking place.

- Prioritizers — people who attempt to assign rankings to alternative future possibilities.

Futurists can also be divided into optimists, pessimists, and incrementalists, which are actually reflections of individual personality rather than necessarily proclaimed statements of personal philosophy (see chapter 1).

Unfortunately, but understandably, no generally accepted definition of the futures field exists. Roy Amara, president of the Institute for the Future, prefers the term *the futures field* to all others (futurism, futurology, futuristics) because it is intended to be broader than, and to encompass, future studies and futures research. Amara, while he is resistant to definitions, is willing to state a few ground rules:

1. **The future is not predictable.** By this he means that there is always uncertainty in anything we do, and it is not the job of the futurist to make oracular predictions, but merely to anticipate changes and plan accordingly.

2. **The future is not predetermined.** Nothing is fixed, nothing is inevitable. Otherwise, why bother?

3. **Future outcomes can be influenced by individual choices.** This means that we have some power to have some influence on future directions, even if only slightly. "No guarantee can be made, of course," says Amara, "that the exercise of choice will produce the desired outcome or even increase or decrease its likelihood."[2]

So what are the goals of the futures field? To conceive and describe perceptions of the future (the possible). To study likely alternatives and particular paths (the probable). And, to express preferences and make choices to bring about a particular feature or to follow a particular path (the preferable). While this may sound simplistic, it is what futurists do, and what each of us, if we train our minds to think in these ways, can do on our own without advanced degrees or affiliation with any institution.

As was stated in chapter 3, there are tools and methodologies for futuring, just as there are for most other areas of inquiry. Among the futurist's bag of tricks are the following:

- an open mind
- pooled intuitive judgment
- thoughtful reading, especially of science fiction and fantasy
- computer simulation and modeling
- gaming and role-playing
- scenario writing and discussion

The futures field comes under fire frequently from people who don't understand its structure, its limitations, and its procedures. Critics worry that there are no criteria for distinguishing "good and useful" futurist work from "bad and misleading" work. This state of affairs angers some critics and causes others to dismiss futurists as visionaries, cranks, and frauds not to be taken seriously by the scientific community. There are, however, certain scientific "litmus tests" of good work. In keeping with accepted scientific rigor, good futures work will avoid giving the impression of prescience and will make explicit the following:

- the futurist's basic premises and assumptions
- the specific purposes of the activity or investigation
- the principal values espoused by the researchers
- the processes and methods used to achieve results
- the tradeoffs requisite in change
- a description of change processes to achieve stated ends (how are we going to get from here to there?)
- the time available to act
- the identification of the product, clear and specific
- the product's credibility
- the product's intended change in perceptions or actions
- the plausibility of the product
- the reproducibility of the process

The ultimate value of all futuring endeavor lies in the amount of faith and belief that people are willing to place in its methods, investigators, conclusions, and implications. As previously stated, everyone is already a futurist and everyone can employ many of the methods of futurists. A few simple procedural rules include:

1. *Identify.* Define the area or institution for which you seek to choose a future or an array of alternative futures.

2. *Describe.* Seek information. What possibilities and choices about the future (of a given field, place, person, group, etc.) exist? Attempt to identify *all* possible directions, including backward, downward, and standing still. Be sure to include as many best cases, worst cases, and change cases as you can.

3. *Measure.* What do we know about our choices, how likely is each to affect our futures and our lifestyles, and in what ways? What are the downside risks of each alternative? Can we anticipate and visualize a world in which each is operating? It is at this phase that the method of scenarios is most productive and fruitful. It lets you try a given future on for size *before* you begin making payments on it.

4. *Judge.* What do you prefer to happen and why? Evaluate each potential future based on the needs of the group, not merely on your own personal wishes. It is sometimes difficult and awkward to set aside purely personal preferences in favor of group benefit, but a measure of altruism is a requisite of the successful futurist. Don't forget costs are a significant constraint. The solution to global air pollution, for example, may be neat, logical, plausible, but out of reach in terms of dollars, rubles, and yen.

5. *Select.* How can you most productively work toward achievement of the most desirable goals or results? Include as many steps along the pathway from here to there as you can. Better to have thought of it early than to realize that you forgot it, omitted it as trivial, or simply left it out at some later date.

It is the author's advice and recommendation that one can get started the easy way by writing a few scenarios. Never mind literary quality, at least at the beginning. Just tell what happens, when, and how each development affects everything else at the time and everything that is to come. Also, ability to write down one's thoughts in a cogent, readable style is a variable spread randomly and unevenly throughout any population, even among academics. Collaboration of thinkers and writers may be recommended.

The bottom line is that if you refuse to make a start, out of inertia or fear of ridicule, nothing is achieved. Write a scenario for your public library, your field, or your nation, however primitive, and you're beginning. Polish it a few times until you dare to show it to another person. Get that person's insights and constructive criticism. Then write another, alternative scenario for the same institution, field of study, or country. Then write another until the possibilities are exhausted. For keeping track, it might be profitable to think of the scenarios as best case, worst case, most desirable, etc. Then go watch a movie on television or go for a walk. By the time you return to thinking about your problem, you should find another scenario or two kicking around in your head. After giving each of your scenarios as much creative, original thought as you can, and discussing them with informed, unbiased colleagues, make a choice, selecting the one you find to be the most preferable, in all major respects. Factor in costs, financial, intellectual, and psychological, and consider who might be opposed to your plan, why, and what difference that might make. Then work conscientiously towards your chosen scenario, paying special attention to the details of how you get from here to there. A word of caution: if you fail to provide intermediate steps your ladder of thought will collapse of its own weight.

What? Are you still sitting there reading? Get over to your typewriter or microcomputer and start writing scenarios. If you do, you have just taken an action in the general direction of improved futures and broader choices among alternatives. If you don't, you have nothing to lose but your freedom of choice and no one to blame but yourself.

> If we don't solve our own problems, other people will—
> and the world of tomorrow belongs to the people who
> will solve them.
>
> —Pierre Elliott Trudeau

NOTES

1. Marvin Cetron and Thomas O'Toole, *Encounters with the Future: A Forecast of Life into the 21st Century* (New York: McGraw-Hill, 1982).

2. Roy Amara, "The Futures Field: Searching for Definitions and Boundaries," *The Futurist* 15 (February 1981): 25-29.

Bibliography

Amara, Roy. "The Futures Field: Searching for Definitions and Boundaries." *The Futurist* 15 (February 1981): 25-29.

Asimov, Isaac. *Change: 71 Glimpses of the Future.* Boston: Houghton-Mifflin, 1981.

Back, Jonathan, and Susan S. Lang. "Holography: Changing the Way We See the World." *The Futurist* 19 (December 1985): 25-28.

Baer, John. "Artificial Intelligence: Making Machines That Think." *The Futurist* 22 (January-February 1988): 8-18.

Ballard, Thomas H. "Technology and the Public Library." *Journal of Educational Media and Library Sciences* 23 (Autumn 1986): 11-21.

Bearman, Toni Carbo. "The Information Society of the 1990s; Blue Sky and Green Pastures?" *Online* 11 (January 1987): 82-86.

Berry, John. "Too Much Technology?" *Library Journal* 111 (January 1986): 4.

Best, Fred. "Technology and the Changing World of Work." *The Futurist* 18 (April 1984): 61-66.

_____. "Recycled People: Work Sharing through Flexible Life Scheduling." *The Futurist* 12 (February 1978): 5-18.

Bezold, Clement, and Robert L. Olson. "The Future of Florida: Four Scenarios for the Sunshine State." *The Futurist* 17 (October 1983): 12-20.

Block, Robert S. "A Global Information Utility." *The Futurist* 18 (December 1984): 31.

Blodgett, Terrell. "The City in 2000 A.D.: A Microcosm of American Democracy." *Public Library Quarterly* 17 (Fall/Winter 1986): 9-25.

Books in Our Future: Perspectives and Proposals, Washington, D.C.: The Library of Congress, 1987.

Boss, Richard W. "Technology and the Modern Library." *Library Journal* 109 (June 15, 1984): 1183-89.

Branwyn, Gareth. "Gaming/Simulating Future Realities." *The Futurist* 20 (January-February 1986): 29-35.

Brill, Louis M. "Planetarium Theaters: The 'Playhouse of the Stars' May Hit the Big Time." *The Futurist* 16 (December 1982): 27-33.

Brousseau, Ray. *Looking Forward*. New York: American Heritage Publishing Company, 1970.

Brown, Arnold. "Equipping Ourselves for the Communications Age." *The Futurist* 15 (August 1981): 53-57.

Buckland, Michael. "Education in the Next Century." *Library Trends* 34 (Spring 1986): 778-87.

Bush, Vannevar. "As We May Think." *Atlantic Monthly* 176 (July 1945): 101-08.

Bylinksy, Gene. "Invasion of the Service Robots." *Fortune* 116 (September 14, 1987): 81-88.

Cetron, Marvin J. "Getting Ready for the Jobs of the Future." *The Futurist* 17 (June 1983): 15-23.

Cetron, Marvin, and Thomas O'Toole. *Encounters with the Future: A Forecast of Life into the 21st Century*. New York: McGraw-Hill, 1982.

Charbeneau, Travis. "Detroit: 2037." *Michigan: The Magazine of the Detroit News* (February 22, 1987): 9- .

Cherlin, A., and F. F. Furstenberg, Jr. "The American Family in the Year 2000." *The Futurist* 17 (June 1983): 7-14.

Childers, Thomas. "Community and Library: Some Possible Futures." *Library Journal* 96 (September 15, 1971): 2727-30.

Chisholm, Margaret E. "Visionary Leaders for 2020: Developing Leadership in Human Resources for Library and Information Science." Inaugural Address, July 1, 1987. Chicago, American Library Association, 1987.

Clarke, Arthur C. *Arthur C. Clarke's July 20, 2019: Life in the 21st Century.* New York: Macmillan, 1986.

Coates, Vary T. "The Potential Impacts of Robotics." *The Futurist* 17 (February 1983): 28-32.

Coleman, D. "The Book ... Is It Terminal?" *New Library World* 85 (November 1984): 189.

Cordell, Arthur J. "Work in the Information Age." *The Futurist* 19 (December 1985): 12-14.

Corn, Joseph J., and Brian Horrigan. *Yesterday's Tomorrows: Past Visions of the American Future.* New York: Summit Books, 1984.

Cornish, Blake M. "The Smart Machines of Tomorrow: Implications for Society." *The Futurist* 15 (August 1981): 5-13.

Cornish, Edward. "The Coming of an Information Society." *The Futurist* 15 (April 1981): 14-22.

_____. "Creating a Better Future: The Role of the World Future Society." *The Futurist* 14 (October 1980): 15-20.

_____. "The Race for Artificial Intelligence." *The Futurist* 19 (June 1985).

_____. "Towards a Philosophy of Futurism." *The Futurist* 11 (December 1977): 380-85.

_____. "What Shall We Call the Study of the Future?" *The Futurist* 11 (February 1977): 44-50.

Craver, Kathleen W. "The Future of School Library Media Centers." *School Library Media Quarterly* 12 (Summer 1984): 266-84.

Crismond, Linda. "The Future of Public Library Services." *Library Journal* 111 (November 15, 1986): 42-49.

de Gennaro, Richard. "Libraries, Technology, and the Information Marketplace." *Library Journal* 107 (June 1982): 1045-54.

"Denvermetro in the 21st Century." First National Bank of Denver, Denver, Colo., 1972. (pamphlet)

Dickson, Paul. *The Future File.* New York: Rawson Associates, 1977.

Diebold, John. "Future View: New Challenges for the Information Age." *The Futurist* 19 (June 1985): 68.

Ditlea, Steve. "The Big Link: Artificial Intelligence." *Omni* 9 (September 1987): 16- .

Dowlin, Kenneth E. "The Electronic Eclectic Library." *Library Journal* 105 (November 1, 1980): 2265-70.

_____. "The Knowledge Center." *Public Library Quarterly* 7 (Fall/Winter 1986): 5-7.

_____. "The Library in 2020." *Public Library Quarterly* 7 (Spring/Summer 1986): 3-9.

Dunn, Samuel L. "The Changing University: Survival in the Information Society." *The Futurist* 17 (August 1983): 55-60.

Dutton, William H., et al., eds. *Wired Cities: Shaping the Future of Communications*. Boston: G. K. Hall, 1987.

Eder, Peter F. "Telecommuters: The Stay-at-Home Work Force of the Future." *The Futurist* 17 (June 1983): 30-31.

Edmunds, Stahrl. "Which Way America? Six Scenarios for the Future of the United States." *The Futurist* 13 (February 1979): 5-12.

Ehrlich, Paul R. *The Population Bomb*. New York: Ballantine Books, 1968.

Ehrlich, Paul R., and Jonathan Roughgarden. *The Science of Ecology*. New York: Macmillan, 1987.

Etzioni, Amitai. "Futures Analysis." In *Libraries in Post-Industrial Society*, edited by Leigh Estabrook, 37-44. Phoenix, Ariz.: The Oryx Press, 1977.

"The Fantastic Future of Albert Robida; The Twentieth Century as Viewed by a Nineteenth-Century Artist." *The Futurist* 19 (August 1985): 46-47.

Fayen, Emily Gallup. "Beyond Technology: Rethinking 'Librarian.'" *American Libraries* 17 (April 1986): 240-42.

Ferkiss, Victor C. *Futurology: Promise, Performance, Prospects*. The Washington Papers, vol. v. Washington, D.C.: The Center for Strategic and International Studies, 1977.

"Five Potential Crises," Trend Analysis Program, American Council of Life Insurance. *The Futurist* 18 (April 1984): 9-20.

Fleming, Don B. "Teaching the Great Issues of the Future." *The Futurist* 21 (January-February, 1987): 27-28.

Fowles, Jib. *Handbook of Futures Research*. Westport, Conn.: Greenwood Press, 1978.

Freedman, Henry B. "Paper's Role in an Electronic World." *The Futurist* 15 (October 1981): 11-16.

Freeman, Michael, and Gary P. Mulkowski. "Advanced Interactive Technology: Robots in the Home and Classroom." *The Futurist* 12 (December 1978): 356-62.

Future of the Book: New Technologies in Book Distribution; The United States Experience: A Report. Paris: UNESCO, 1984. (fiche)

"The Futurists: Looking toward A.D. 2000." *Time* 87 (February 25, 1966): 28-29.

Gallup, George. *Forecast 2000: George Gallup, Jr. Predicts the Future of America.* New York: Morrow, 1984.

Garfield, Eugene. "2001: An Information Society?" *Journal of Information Science* 1 (October 1979): 209-15.

Giuliano, Vincent E. "A Manifesto for Librarians." *Library Journal* 104 (September 15, 1979): 1837-42.

Gleave, D., C. Angell, and K. Woolley. "Structural Change within the Information Profession: A Scenario for the 1990s." *ASLIB Proceedings* 37 (February 1985): 99-133.

"Global 2000 Report Paints Stark Picture." *The Futurist* 14 (October 1980): 58-61.

Grant, Lindsey. "The Cornucopian Fallacies: The Myth of Perpetual Growth." *The Futurist* 17 (August 1983): 16-22.

Griffen, Agnes M. "Images of Libraries in Science Fiction." *Library Journal* 112 (September 1, 1987): 137-42.

Hald, Alan P. "Toward the Information-Rich Society." *The Futurist* 15 (August 1981): 20-24.

Harmon, George H. "Micrographs: Return of the 25-Cent Book?" *The Futurist* 15 (October 1981): 61-66.

Heydinger, Richard B., and René D. Zentner. "Multiple Scenario Analysis: Introducing Uncertainty into the Planning Process." In *Applying Methods and Techniques of Futures Research*, edited by James L. Morrison et al., 51-68. San Francisco: Jossey-Bass, Inc., 1983.

Higgins, Mike. "The Future of Personal Robots." *The Futurist* 20 (May-June 1986): 43-47.

Hoadley, Irene. "The World That Awaits Us: Libraries of Tomorrow." *Wilson Library Bulletin* 61 (October 1986): 22-25.

Hoban, Phoebe. "Disc-O-Tech: Artificial Intelligence." *Omni* 8 (August 1986): 24- .

Hopkins, Frank Snowden. "Communication: The Civilizing Force." *The Futurist* 15 (April 1981): 39-40.

Hubbard, Barbara Marx. "The Future of Futurism: Creating a New Synthesis." *The Futurist* 17 (April 1983): 52-58.

Hurly, Paul. "The Promises and Perils of Videotex." *The Futurist* 19 (April 1985): 7-14.

"An Inquiry into George Orwell's 1984." *The Futurist* 17 (December 1983).

Jacobs, Madeline. "Yesterday's Predictions: The Way the Future Was." *The Futurist* 19 (February 1985): 42-45.

Jennings, Lane. "The Human Side of Tomorrow's Communications." *The Futurist* 13 (April 1979): 104-9.

_____. "Why Books Will Survive." *The Futurist* 17 (April 1983): 5-11.

Johansen, Robert, Jacques Vallee, and Kathleen Spangler. "Electronic Meetings: Utopian Dreams and Complex Realities." *The Futurist* 12 (October 1978): 313-20.

Kagan, Daniel. "PSI for Hire." *Omni* 6 (September 1984): 20.

"Kahn, Mead, and Thompson: A Three-Way Debate on the Future." *The Futurist* 12 (August 1978): 229-32.

Kilgour, Frederick G. "EIDOS and the Transformation of Libraries." *Library Journal* 112 (October 1, 1987): 46-49.

Kirby, M. D. "The Morning Star of Informatics Law and the Need for a Greater Sense of Urgency." *Government Publications Review* (May/June 1985): 203-14.

Klopfenstein, Bruce C. "Forecasting Use of Home Information Technologies." *Bulletin of the American Society for Information Science* 12 (October/November 1986): 16-17.

Knauer, Gene. "Computer Programs for the Mind: New Ways to Learn." *The Futurist* 20 (March-April 1986): 33-35.

Kotler, Philip. "'Dream Vacations': The Booming Market in Designed Experiences." *The Futurist* 18 (October 1984): 713.

Kountz, John. "Robots in the Library: Automated Storage and Retrieval Systems." *Library Journal* 112 (December 1987): 67-70.

Kroger, Joseph J. "Artificial Intelligence: A New Reality." *The Futurist* 21 (July-August 1987): 38-40.

Lamm, Richard D. *Megatraumas: America at the Year 2000*. Boston: Houghton-Mifflin, 1985.

Lancaster, F. W. "Future Librarianship: Preparing for an Unconventional Career." *Wilson Library Bulletin* 57 (May 1983): 748-53.

_____. "The Paperless Society Revisited." *American Libraries* 16 (September 1985): 553-55.

Landrum, Suzanne. "Will There Be a Library for Your Future?" *Public Library Quarterly* 6 (Spring 1985): 7-11.

Leinwald, Gerald, ed. *The Future*. New York: Pocket Books, 1976.

Lewis, Dennis A. "Today's Challenge—Tomorrow's Choice: Change or Be Changed or The Doomsday Scenario Mk.2." *Journal of Information Science* 2 (September 1980): 59-74.

Libraries 2000: A Futures Symposium. Toronto: The Ontario Ministry of Citizenship and Culture, 1985.

Licklider, J. C. R. *Libraries of the Future*. Cambridge, Mass.: The M.I.T. Press, 1965.

Lipnack, Jessica, and Jeffrey Stamps. "A Network Model." *The Futurist* 21 (July-August 1987): 23-25.

London, Herbert I. "Death of the University." *The Futurist* 21 (May-June 1987): 17-22.

Long, Sandra M., and Winston H. Long. "Rethinking Video Games: A New Challenge." *The Futurist* 18 (December 1984): 35-37.

Loye, David. "The Forecasting Brain: How We See the Future." *The Futurist* 18 (February 1984): 63-68.

Macrae, Norman. *The 2025 Report: A Concise History of the Future, 1975-2025*. New York: Macmillan, 1984.

Marien, Michael. "The Good News and the Bad News: Optimism vs. Pessimism in Recent Writing about the Future." *The Futurist* 14 (June 1980): 310.

Markley, O. W. "Preparing for the Professional Futures Field: Observations from the UHCLC Futures Program." *Futures* 15 (February 1983): 47-64.

Martino, Joseph P. "Telecommunications in the Year 2000." *The Futurist* 13 (April 1979): 95-103.

Marx, Gary T. "The Surveillance Society: The Threat of 1984-Style Techniques." *The Futurist* 19 (June 1985): 21-26.

Mason, Ellsworth. "Along the Academic Way." *Library Journal* 96 (May 15, 1971): 1675.

Mason, Marilyn Gell. "The Future of the Public Library." *Library Journal* 110 (September 1, 1985): 136-39.

Mason, Roy, Lane Jennings, and Robert Evans. "A Day at Xanadu: Family Life in Tomorrow's Computerized Home." *The Futurist* 18 (February 1984): 17-25.

McCrackin, Mark. "Just Imagine ... The Implications of Technological Changes in Computing and Telecommunications." *Top of the News* 39 (Summer 1983): 347-51.

Moore, Dan T., Jr. "Will Robots Save Democracy?" *The Futurist* 15 (August 1981): 14-19.

Morf, Martin. "Eight Scenarios for Work in the Future." *The Futurist* 17 (June 1983): 24-29.

Morrison, Elizabeth. "Futures Research in Librarianship." *Library Research* (Fall 1980): 195-213.

Morrison, Perry R. "Computer Parasites; Software Diseases May Cripple Our Computers." *The Futurist* 20 (March-April 1986): 36-38.

Naisbitt, John. *Megatrends: Ten Directions Transforming Our Lives*. New York: Warner Books, 1982.

Neill, S. D. "Libraries in 2010: The Information Brokers." *The Futurist* 15 (October 1981): 47-60.

Novak, Michael. "The World in 2010." *Vital Speeches of the Day* (June 15, 1985): 538-42.

O'Neill, Gerard K. *2081: A Hopeful View of the Human Future*. New York: Simon & Schuster, 1981.

Otto, Theophil. "The Academic Librarian of the 21st Century: Public Service and Library Education in the Year 2000." *Journal of Academic Librarianship* 8 (June 1982): 85-88.

Paisley, William J. "Electronic Information and the Library's Public." In *Online Catalogs, Online Reference*, edited by Brian Aveny. Chicago: American Library Association, 1984.

Parnes, Sidney J. "Learning Creative Behavior: Making the Future Happen." *The Futurist* 18 (August 1984): 30-32.

Petroski, Henry. "The Electronic Newspaper: An Easy Route to 1984." *The Futurist* 16 (August 1982): 59-60.

Porter, Alan. "Work in the Information Age." *The Futurist* 20 (September-October 1986): 9-15.

Raloff, Janet. "Coming: The Big Chill?" *Science News* 131 (May 16, 1987): 314-17.

Rice, James G. "The Dream of the Memex." *American Libraries* 19 (January 1988): 14-17.

_____. "Telereference Services: The Potential for Libraries." *Library Journal* 108 (October 1, 1983): 1839-43.

"Robots and Job Loss; Few Workers Will Be Displaced." *The Futurist* 19 (April 1985): 73.

Rochell, Carlton. "Telematics—2001 AD." *Library Journal* 107 (October 1982): 1809-15.

Roland, Jon. "The Microelectronic Revolution: How Intelligence on a Chip Will Change Our Lives." *The Futurist* 13 (April 1979): 81-90.

Rossman, Parker. "The Coming Great Electronic Encyclopedia." *The Futurist* 16 (August 1982): 53-57.

Saunders, A. W. "Big Brother or Space Odyssey? Public Librarianship—The Next Decade and Beyond." *SLA News* no. 184 (November/December 1984): 24-27.

Shane, Harold G., and Gary A. Sojka. "John Elfreth Watkins, Jr., Forgotten Genius of Forecasting." *The Futurist* 16 (October 1982): 8-14.

Sharr, F. A. "The Public Library: Dodo or Phoenix." *Libri* 24 (1974): 89-101.

Simon, Julian L. "Life on Earth Is Getting Better, Not Worse." *The Futurist* 17 (August 1983): 7-14.

Smith, Robert Frederick. "A Funny Thing Is Happening to the Library on Its Way to the Future." *The Futurist* 12 (April 1978): 85-91.

"Son of Brave New World: An Interview with Matthew Huxley." *The Futurist* 19 (December 1985): 15-18.

Stueart, Robert D. "Preparing Libraries for Change." *Library Journal* 109 (September 15, 1984): 1724-26.

Sugnet, Chris. "Education and Automation—Present and Future Concerns." *Library Hi Tech* (Issue 18): 105-12.

Surprenant, Thomas. "Future Libraries." *Wilson Library Bulletin* (an occasional column of fact, theory, and opinion). Articles consulted:

    1982:   (January) 336-41. (October) 152-53. (December) 328-29.

    1983:   (February) 499+. (May) 764-65, 99. (June) 852-53. (October) 126-27.

    1984:   (April) 574-75.

    1987:   (January) 52-53.

Surprenant, Thomas T., and Claudia Perry-Holmes. "The Reference Librarian of the Future: A Scenario." *Reference Quarterly* 25 (Winter 1985): 234-38.

Toffler, Alvin. *The Eco-spasm Report*. New York: Bantam, 1975.

_____. *Future Shock*. New York: Random House, 1971.

_____. *Previews and Premises*. New York: Random House, 1983.

_____. *The Third Wave*. New York: Morrow, 1980.

Trezza, Alphonse F., ed. *Public Libraries and the Challenges of the Next Two Decades*. Littleton, Colo.: Libraries Unlimited, Inc., 1985.

Tydeman, John. "Videotex: Ushering in the Electronic Household." *The Futurist* (February 1982): 54-62.

Vail, Hollis. "The Home Computer Terminal: Transforming the Household of Tomorrow." *The Futurist* 14 (December 1980): 52-58.

Vaughan, Alan. "Intuition, Precognition, and the Art of Prediction." *The Futurist* 16 (June 1982): 510.

Vavrek, Bernard. "The Future of Rural Libraries." *Rural Libraries* 2 (Winter 1982): 55-66.

Wagar, W. Warren. "Toward a World Set Free: The Vision of H. G. Wells." *The Futurist* 17 (August 1983): 24-31.

Wakefield, Rowan A. "Home Computers & Families: The Empowerment Revolution." *The Futurist* 20 (September-October 1986): 18-23.

Wallechinsky, David, et al. *The Book of Predictions*. New York: Morrow, 1980.

Watstein, Sarah, and Martin Kesselman. "In Pursuit of Artificial Intelligence." *Library Hi Tech News*. Issue no. 30 (September 1986).

Weiner, Edith, and Arthur Brown. "Issues for the 1990s." *The Futurist* 20 (March/April 1986).

"What the Next 50 Years Will Bring." *U.S. News & World Report* 94 (May 9, 1983): A-1-A-42.

"Why Forecasters Flubbed the '70s." *Time* 115 (January 21, 1980): 91-92.

Wolfgram, Tammara H. "Working at Home: The Growth of Cottage Industry." *The Futurist* 18 (June 1984): 31-34.

Index